Timeless Treasures

Selected by
VERNON MCLELLAN

THOMAS NELSON PUBLISHERS
Nashville • Atlanta • London • Vancouver

Published in Nashville, tennessee, by Thomas Nelson, Inc., Publishers , and distributed in Canada by Word Communications, Ltd., Richmond, British Columbia, and in the United Kingdom by Word (UK), Ltd., Milton Keynes, England.

Unless otherwise noted, Scripture quotations are from The Living Bible (Wheaton, Illinois: Tyndale House Publishers, 1971) and are used by permission.

Scripture quotations noted NASB are from THE NEW AMERICAN STANDARD BIBLE, Copyright© 1960, 1962, 1963, 1968, 1971 1972, 1973, 1975, 1977 by The Lockman Foundation and are used by permission.

Scripture quotations noted NIV are taken from the HOLY BIBLE, NEW INTERNATIONAL VERSION ©. Copyright© 1973, 1978, 1984, by International Bible Society. Used by permission of Zondervan Bible Publishing House. All rights reserved.

The "NIV" and "New International Version" trademarks are registered in the United States Patent and Trademark Office by International Bible Society. Use of either trademark requires the permission of International Bible Society.

Scripture quotations noted NKJV are from THE NEW KING JAMES VERSION. Copyright© 1979, 1980, 1982, Thomas Nelson, Inc., Publishers.

Scripure quotations noted RSV are from the REVISED STANDARD VERSION of the Bible. Copyright © 1946, 1952, 1971, 1973 by the Division of Christian Education of the National Coucil of the Churches of Christ in the U.S.A. Used by permission.

Library of Congress Cataloging-in-Publication Data

McLellan, Vernon K.

   Timeless treasures / selected by Vernon McLellan.

      p. cm.

   Originally published: San Bernardino, CA : Here's Life Publishers, 1992

   ISBN 0-8407-3508-1 (hc)

   1. Quotations, English. 2. Quotations, American. I. Title.

PN6081.M467 1994

082—dc20   94-16441

                               CIP

Printed in the United States of America

2 3 4 5 6 7 8 —99 98 97 96 95 94

Contents

To my beloved parents,
who taught me early in life
the value of a word of wisdom
wrapped up in a quotation.

Introduction

"I quote others to better express myself," admitted Michel de Montaigne. And that's how I feel. "When you take stuff from one writer it's plagiarism," wrote Wilson Mizner, "but when you take it from many writers, it's research."

Sir Henry Wotton and I have the same opinion: "I am but a gatherer and disposer of other men's stuff." I've been doing this "research" since I was a kid—and have loved every minute of it!

Sir James Mackintosh declared that "maxims are the condensed good sense of nations." We need more good sense (common sense)—an uncommon commodity anymore! In *Timeless Treasures* you'll find hundreds of maxims, quotations and proverbs that I've found in scores of places through the years. Jesus was a master one-liner and of course has been quoted countless times. His one-sentence statements stick to our minds. "Render unto Caesar the things that are Caesar's and unto God the things that are God's." A powerful, gripping statement.

Or, "Blessed are the meek for they shall inherit the earth." How about Matthew 7:7? "Ask, and it shall be given you; seek, and ye shall find; knock, and it shall be opened unto you."

John 3:16 has been tagged "The Gospel in a Nutshell." "For God so loved the world, that he gave his only begotten Son, that whosoever believeth in him should not perish, but have everlasting life."

What about Matthew 5:9? "Blessed are the peacemakers: for they shall be called the children of God."

Here are several suggestions for enjoying this book, making it useful, and drawing out its maximum benefit:

1. Memorize key lines; reduce them to 3 x 5 cards; stick them in your pocket or purse and refer to them at opportune moments.

2. Start public or private school sessions with one or two quotes on the chalkboard; make them a point of discussion.

3. Use them as a P.S. on a letter.

4. Ask your students (young and old) to interpret a quotation for the group.

5. Make a calligraphic or normal poster out of a one-liner.

6. A writer, teacher or preacher can include quotations in their communications to others.

7. As you start and end the day, use a few of them as inspirational, instructional thoughts in personal devotions.

8. A manager could use motivational statements to begin a sales meeting.

Using your imagination, apply these timely truths to everyday situations. Both you and the one "getting the message" will be richer for it.

VERNON MCLELLAN
CHARLOTTE, NORTH CAROLINA

These *Timeless Treasures* have been gathered from
many sources—most do not have a byline. If you
recognize any of these and know the author, please
send his (her) name to me in care of the publisher.
We will add that name to a future edition of this
book. Thank you for your help.

The author

Accomplishment
(also Achievement)

High Flight

Oh! I have slipped the surly bonds of earth
And danced the skies on laughter-silvered wings;
Sunward I've climbed, and joined the tumbling mirth
Of sun-split clouds—and done a hundred things
You have not dreamed of—wheeled and soared and
    swung
High in the sunlit silence. Hov'ring there,
I've chased the shouting wind along, and flung
My eager craft through footless halls of air.

Up, up the long, delirious, burning blue
I've topped the wind-swept heights with easy grace
Where never lark, or even eagle flew—
And, while with silent lifting mind I've trod
The high untrespassed sanctity of space,
Put out my hand and touched the face of God.
                        —*John Gillespie Magee, Jr.*

If God simply handed us everything we wanted,
He'd be taking from us our greatest prize—the joy of
accomplishment.

Your Best Foot Forward

Which sounds longer to you, 569,400 hours or 65
years? They are exactly the same in length of time.
The average man spends his first eighteen years—
157,000 hours—getting an education. That leaves
him 412,000 hours from age 18 to 65. Eight hours of
every day are spent in sleeping; eight hours in eating
and recreation. So there is left eight hours to work
in each day. One third of 412,000 hours is 134,000
hours—the number of hours a man has in which to
work between the age of 18 and 65. Expressed in
hours it doesn't seem a very long time, does it? Now
I am not recommending that you tick off the hours
that you worked, 134,000, 133,999, 133,990, etc., but
I do suggest that whatever you do, you do it with all
that you have in you. If you are sleeping, sleep well.
If you are playing, play well. If you are working, give
the best that is in you, remembering that in the last
analysis the real satisfactions in life come not from
money and things, but from the realization of a job
well done. Therein lies the difference between the
journeyman worker and a real craftsman.

—*H. W. Prentis, Jr.*

There are four steps to accomplishment: First, plan purposefully; second, prepare prayerfully; third, proceed positively; fourth, pursue persistently.

Our Unfinished World

God gave us a world unfinished, so we might share
 in the joys and satisfactions of creation.
He left oil in Trenton rock.
He left electricity in the clouds.
He left the rivers unbridged—and the mountains
 untrailed.
He left the forests unfelled and the cities unbuilt.
He left the laboratories unopened.
He left the diamonds uncut.
He gave us the challenge of raw materials, not the
 satisfaction of perfect, finished things.
He left the music unsung and the dramas unplayed.
He left the poetry undreamed, in order that men and
 women might not become bored, but engage in
 stimulating, exciting, creative activities that keep
 them thinking, working, experimenting, and
 experiencing all the joys and durable satisfactions
 of achievement.

—Allen A. Stockdale

After all is said and done, there's more said than done.

Unless you try to do something beyond what you
have already mastered, you will never grow.
                                    —*Ronald E. Osborn*

Do not mistake activity for achievement.

If you wait for perfect conditions, you will never get
anything done . . . Keep on sowing your seed, for
you never know which will grow—perhaps it all will.
                        —*Solomon (Ecclesiastes 11:4,6)*

There is no limit to what can be accomplished if it
doesn't matter who gets the credit.
                                    —*Ralph Waldo Emerson*

He who thinks by the inch and talks by the yard
deserves to be kicked by the foot.

You can't build your reputation on what you're going
to do.   —*Henry Ford*

Every day you write your own paycheck.
                                    —*Alfred Montapert*

Far away there in the sunshine are my highest aspira-
tions. I may not reach them but I can look up and see
their beauty, believe in them and try to follow where
they lead.   —*Louisa May Alcott*

You will become as small as your controlling desire;
as great as your dominant aspiration.   *—James Allen*

Definiteness of purpose is the starting point of all
achievement.   *—Clement Stone*

The three great essentials to achieve anything worthwhile are first, hard work; second, stick-to-itiveness;
third, common sense.   *—Thomas Edison*

When your adversaries tell you that you can't go any
further, just tell them to look behind you and see
how far you've come.

It's not what you'll do when you're older,
tomorrow, next week or next year,
But what you accomplish or finish
before tonight's shadows draw near;
For nothing is gained on the morrow,
for work then no one draws pay,
So earnestly strive to accomplish
the task one should finish each day.
                                    —Alonzo Newton Benn

The most agreeable thing in life is worthy accomplishment.   *—Edgar Rowe*

No matter what your lot in life, build something on it.

Lord, grant that I may always desire more than I can accomplish.   —*Michelangelo*

He who wants to make a place in the sun should expect blisters.

Every man who is high up loves to think he has done it all himself; and his wife smiles, and lets it go at that.   —*James Barrie*

The Difficult is that which can be done immediately; The Impossible that which takes a little longer.
                                          —*George Santayana*

The only people who achieve much are those who want knowledge so badly that they seek it while the conditions are still unfavorable. Favorable conditions never come.   —*C. S. Lewis*

He who putters around winds up in the hole.

If your mind can conceive it, and your heart can believe it, then you can achieve it.

Listen to me! You can pray for anything, and, if you believe you have it, it's yours.   —*Jesus (Mark 11:24)*

Some fellows dream of worthy accomplishment, while others stay awake and experience it.

I have fought the good fight, I have finished the course, I have kept the faith.
—*The Apostle Paul (2 Timothy 4:7)*

Action
(also Initiative)

One hour of life, crowded to the full with glorious action, and filled with noble risks, is worth whole years of those mean observances of paltry decorum, in which men steal through existence, like sluggish waters through a marsh, without either honor or observation. —*Sir Walter Scott*

Talking with humorist Mark Twain, a man commented that his greatest ambition was to visit Mt. Sinai and there see the place where God gave Moses the Ten Commandments.

Mark Twain responded by saying, "Why don't you just stay home and keep the Ten Commandments?"

It doesn't do a man any good to sit up and take notice if he keeps on sitting.

Initiative is doing the right thing at the right time without having to be told.

Between saying and doing many a pair of shoes is worn out.   —*Italian proverb*

I have never heard anything about the resolutions of the apostles, but I have heard a great deal about the acts of the apostles.

Whatsoever thy hand findeth to do, do it with thy might.   —*Solomon (Ecclesiastes 9:10, KJV)*

No one can write his real religious life with pen or pencil. It is written only in actions, and its seal is our character, not our orthodoxy. Whether we, our neighbor, or God is the judge, absolutely the only value of our religious life to ourselves or to anyone is what it fits us for or enables us to do.   —*Wilfred T. Grenfell*

He who is waiting for something to turn up might start with his own shirt sleeves.

People may doubt what you say, but they'll always believe what you do.

Then the Lord said to Moses, "Quit praying and get the people moving! Forward march!"
—*Exodus 14:15*

The more push a person possesses, the less pull he needs. Every great man of God has been a self-starter.

Thinking well is wise; planning well wiser; doing well wisest of all.

Do something. Either lead, follow or get out of the way.
—*Ted Turner*

He who starts a journey of a thousand miles begins with one step.

Even if you're on the right track, you'll get run over if you just sit there.
—*Will Rogers*

I do the best I know how, the very best I can; and I mean to keep on doing it to the end.

If the end brings me out all right, what is said against me will not amount to anything.

If the end brings me out wrong, ten angels swearing I was right would make no difference.
—*Abraham Lincoln*

Don't stand shivering upon the bank; plunge in at once, and have it over.   —*Sam Slick*

Those who act receive the prizes.   —*Aristotle*

God save us from hotheads that would lead us to act foolishly, and from cold feet that would keep us from acting at all.   —*Peter Marshall*

The credit belongs to the man who is actually in the arena, whose face is marred by dust and sweat and blood, who strives valiantly, who errs and comes short again and again, who knows the great enthusiasms, the great devotions, and spends himself in a worthy cause; who at the best, knows the triumph of high achievement; and who, at the worst, if he fails, at least fails while daring greatly, so that his place shall never be with those cold and timid souls who know neither victory nor defeat.

—*Theodore Roosevelt*

People forget how fast you did a job—but they remember how well you did it.

—*Howard W. Newton*

Progress always involves risk; you can't steal second base and keep your foot on first.   —*Frederick Wilcox*

Well done is better than well said.

—*Benjamin Franklin*

Words! Words! Words! I'm so sick of words!
I get words all day through;
First from him, now from you!
Is that all you blighters can do?

Don't talk of stars
Burning above;
If you're in love,
Show me!

Tell me no dreams
Filled with desire.
If you're on fire,
Show me! —*Composer unknown*

It is more important to know where you are going than to get there quickly. Do not confuse action for accomplishment.

You cannot make a place for yourself in the sun if you keep sitting in the shade of the family tree.

Yesterday is a canceled check; tomorrow is a promissory note; today is the only cash you have—so spend it wisely. —*Kay Lyons*

Did is a word of achievement,
Won't is a word of retreat,
Might is a word of bereavement,
Can't is a word of defeat,
Ought is a word of duty,
Try is a word each hour,
Will is a word of beauty,
Can is a word of power.

Roadside sign in Kentucky: "Pray for a good harvest, but keep on hoeing."

Let us then be up and doing,
With a heart for any fate;
Still achieving, still pursuing,
Learn to labor and to wait.   *—Henry W. Longfellow*

The thing to try when all else fails is again. Giving it another try is better than an alibi.

Everything comes to him who hustles while he waits.
                                                    —Thomas Edison

The people who get on in this world are the people who get up and look for the circumstances they want, and, if they can't find them, make them.
                                            —George Bernard Shaw

Don't find fault. Find a remedy.   —*Henry Ford*

He who believes is strong; he who doubts is weak.
Strong convictions precede great actions.
                                          —*J. F. Clarke*

Deliberation is the work of many men. Action, of
one alone.   —*Charles De Gaulle*

No one knows what he can do till he tries.
                                          —*Publius Syrus*

This one thing I do ... I press toward the mark for
the prize of the high calling of God in Christ Jesus.
          —*The Apostle Paul (Philippians 3:13,14, KJV)*

Action should not be confused with haste.
                                          —*Lee Iacocca*

You can't think and hit the ball at the same time.
                         —*Lawrence Peter "Yogi" Berra*

From where you sit, you can probably reach out with
comparative ease and touch a life of serenity and
peace. You can wait for things to happen and not get
too sad when they don't. That's fine for some but
not for me. Serenity is pleasant, but it lacks the
ecstacy of achievement.   —*Estee Lauder*

Adaptability
(also Flexibility, Change, Adjustment)

The most significant change in a person's life is a change of attitude—right attitudes produce right actions.   —*William J. Johnston*

Be not the first by whom the new is tried,
Nor yet the last to lay the old aside.
                                              —*Alexander Pope*

It is well for people to change their minds occasionally in order to keep them clean.   —*Luther Burbank*

Sign on a pastor's desk: "It's too late to agree with me, I've already changed my mind."

The foolish and the dead alone never change their opinions.   —*James R. Lowell*

If you don't like the weather in New England, just wait a few minutes.   —*Mark Twain*

Most people are willing to change, not because they see the light, but because they feel the heat.

When you're through changing, you're through.
—*Bruce Barton*

The past is a guidepost, not a hitching post.
—*L. Thomas Holdcroft*

A wise man changes his mind; a fool never does.

The bamboo which bends is stronger than the oak
which resists.   —*Japanese proverb*

The price of progress is change, and it is taking just
about all we have.

We often grow more by bending than by standing in
rigid defiance.   —*J. Stephens*

Many people hate any change that doesn't jingle in
their pocket.

Alteration is not always improvement, as the pigeon
said when it got out of the net into the pie.
—*Charles Spurgeon*

A young teacher appeared for his first job interview
in a rustic mountain village. The members of the
school board quizzed him thoroughly on the acceptability of his views for their young charges. At last

one of the elders asked, "We have heard a lot of talk that the world is round, while others reckon that it appears to be flat. How do you feel about this?"

The young man, anxious for employment, replied, "I can teach it either way."

The world changes so fast that you couldn't stay wrong all the time if you tried.

Get your facts first, and then you can distort them as much as you please.   —*Mark Twain*

About the only opinions that do not eventually change are the ones we have about ourselves.

There's a small town in Nevada where so little ever changes that the local radio station is still running last year's weather forecasts.

What we want is progress, if we can have it without change.

Everybody thinks of changing humanity and nobody thinks of changing himself.   —*Leo Tolstoy*

People change, fashions change, and conditions change but God never changes.   —*Billy Graham*

Advice

A fool thinks he needs no advice, but a wise man
listens to others.   —*Solomon (Proverbs 12:15)*

Admonish your friends privately, but praise them
openly.   —*Syrus*

The surest way to lose a friend is to tell him something for his own good.   —*Laurie Baker*

If you are old, give advice; if you are young, take it.

He who won't be counseled can't be helped.

One thing I've learned in growing old,
No doubt you've noticed too:
The kids to whom you gave advice
Now give advice to you.   —*F. G. Kernan*

Most people wish to serve God—but only in an
advisory capacity.

The boss looks at me as a sort of consultant; he cold
me when he wants my advice, he'll ask for it.

Advising a fool is like beating the air with a stick.

Football coach to high school team: "Remember, football develops individuality, initiative, and leadership. Now get out there and do exactly what I tell you."

The way to be successful is to follow the advice you give others.

The best way to give advice to your children is find out what they want to do and then advise them to do it.   —*Harry Truman*

Good advice is no better than poor advice, unless you follow it.

Advice: A commodity sold by your lawyer, given freely by your mother-in-law, but impossible to dispose of by yourself.

Where's the man who counsel can bestow
Still pleased to teach, and yet not proud to know?
                                                —*Alexander Pope*

It is not often that any man can have so much knowledge of another as is necessary to make instruction useful.   —*Samuel Johnson*

We may give advice, but we cannot inspire conduct.
—La Rochefoucauld

Advice after injury is like medicine after death.
—Danish proverb

The advice of a wise man refreshes like water from a mountain spring. Those accepting it become aware of the pitfalls on ahead.   *—Solomon (Proverbs 13:14)*

Ambition

Ambition is the spur that makes man struggle with destiny.   *—Donald G. Mitchell*

The seven stages of ambition:
to be like dad;
to be an engineer;
to pilot an airplane;
to be famous;
to become a millionaire;
to make both ends meet;
to hang in long enough to draw a pension.

You Can Touch the Stars
Stars have too long been symbols of the unattainable.
They should not be so. For although our physical
hands cannot reach them, we can touch them in
other ways.

Let stars stand for those things which are ideal and
radiant in life; if we seek sincerely and strive hard
enough, it is possible to reach them, even though the
goals seem distant at the onset.

And how often do we touch stars when we find
them close by in the shining lives of great souls, in
the sparkling universe of humanity around us!
—*Esther Baldwin York*

If a man constantly aspires, is he not elevated?
—*Henry David Thoreau*

A small boy's ambition: to grow up to be a farmer so
he can get paid for not raising spinach.

This should be your ambition: to live a quiet life,
minding your own business and doing your own
work, just as we told you before.
—*The Apostle Paul (1 Thessalonians 4:11)*

Ambition never gets you anywhere until it forms a
partnership with blood, sweat, toil and tears.

There seems to be an ambition on the part of many to learn "the tricks of the trade" rather than the trade.

The Gate of the Year
And I said to the man who stood at the gate of the year: "Give me a light, that I may tread safely into the unknown."

And he replied: "Go out into the darkness and put your hand into the Hand of God. That shall be to you better than light and safer than a known way."

So, I went forth, and finding the Hand of God, trod gladly into the night. And he led me toward the hills and the breaking of the day in the lone East.

So, heart, be still:
What need our little life,
Our human life, to know,
If God hath comprehension?
In all the dizzy strife
Of things both high and low
God hideth His intention.

The first one gets the oyster, the second gets the shell.
—*Andrew Carnegie*

Ambition and death are alike in this: neither is ever satisfied. —*Solomon (Proverbs 27:20)*

He who would rise in the world should veil his ambition with the forms of humanity.   —*Chinese proverb*

Ambition is the drive that always keeps you trying, especially in trying times.

Ambition is a get-ahead-ache.

Ambition is the strong desire in a man to make money, and in a woman to find a man who makes money.

By working faithfully eight hours a day you may eventually get to be a boss and work twelve hours a day.   —*Robert Frost*

Too low they build who build beneath the stars.
                                                   —*Edward Young*

You do not test the resources of God until you attempt the impossible.   —*F. B. Meyer*

Ambition—the drive to succeed so that one will have a happier time in his second childhood than in his first.

If at first you don't succeed, try a little ardor.

An electric light manufacturer approached the theater owner and offered him free bulbs for his marquee in order to satisfy his one great ambition in life.

"I'll take the free bulbs," the theater owner said, "if you tell me what your secret ambition is."

"Sure," said the manufacturer, "I've always dreamed of seeing my lights up in names."

He who would leap high must take a long run.
                                    —*Danish proverb*

Behold the turtle. He makes progress only when he sticks his neck out.   —*James Bryant Conant*

Human beings, like chickens, thrive best when they scratch for what they get.

A man's worth is no greater than the worth of his ambitions.   —*Marcus Aurelius*

Without a doubt, the easiest undertaking to start from scratch is a flea circus.

He who does not hope to win has already lost.
                                    —*Jose Joaquin Olmedo*

Most people would succeed in small things, if they
were not troubled with great ambitions.

—Longfellow

Be wise;
Soar not too high to fall,
but stoop to rise.   *—Philip Massinger*

Though ambition may be a fault in itself, it is often
the mother of virtues.   *—Quintilian*

Keep away from people who try to belittle your ambitions. Small people always do that, but the really
great make you feel that you too can become great.

—Mark Twain

Attitude

A famous conductor said, "The most difficult instru-
ment to play is second fiddle. To find a violinist who
can play second fiddle with enthusiasm—that's a
problem. But if we have no second fiddles, we have
no harmony."

A servant seeks the success of others.

Two men look out through the same bars;
one sees mud, the other sees stars.

Whoever wishes to become great among you shall be
your servant.   —*Jesus Christ (Matthew 20:26, NASB)*

No one is truly literate who cannot read his own
heart.

The most destructive acid in the world is found in a
sour disposition.

There's no danger of developing eyestrain from looking on the bright side of things.

Two bricklayers were asked what they were doing.
The first replied, "I'm laying bricks"; the second
responded, "I'm building a great cathedral." Same
task, different perspective.

Some people grin and bear it. Others smile and
change it.

A relaxed attitude lengthens a man's life; jealousy
rots it away.   —*Solomon (Proverbs 14:30)*

There isn't a person anywhere who isn't capable of
doing more than he thinks he can.   —*Henry Ford*

The loser says, "The worst is just around the corner."
The winner says, "The best is yet to come."

If we did all we are capable of doing we would literally astonish ourselves.   —*Thomas A. Edison*

It isn't hard to make a mountain out of a molehill.
Just add a little dirt.

Here is the ladder to your dreams. The first rung is
determination! And the second rung is dedication!
The third is discipline! And the fourth rung is attitude!
        —*Jesse Owen's coach before*
        the Berlin Olympic Games

Give some weeds an inch and they'll take a yard!

Men can alter their lives by altering their attitudes.
        —*William James*

A man who sits in a swamp all day waiting to shoot
a duck but gripes if his wife has dinner ten minutes
late is a miserable soul.

"Whines" are the products of sour grapes.

To live above with saints we love,
O that will be glory!
To live below with saints we know,
That's a different story.

To one man, the world is barren, dull and superficial,
to another rich, interesting and full of meaning.
—*Schopenhauer*

Our attitude toward life counts more than our
ancestry.   —*Roy L. Smith*

There is very little difference in people but that little
difference makes a big difference. The little difference is attitude. The big difference is whether it is
positive or negative.   —*Clement Stone*

A good thing to remember,
A better thing to do—
Work with the construction gang,
Not with the wrecking crew.

Don't bother to give God instructions; just report for
duty.   —*Corrie ten Boom*

Keep your face to the sunshine and you cannot see
the shadow.   —*Helen Keller*

Assume a cheerfulness you do not feel and shortly you will feel the cheerfulness you assumed.

—*Chinese proverb*

He who wants to sing will find a song.

Worry never robs tomorrow of its sorrow; it only saps today of its strength.   —*A. J. Cronin*

Attitudes determine our altitudes.

In War: Resolution. In Defeat: Defiance. In Victory: Magnanimity. In Peace: Goodwill.

—*Sir Winston Churchill*

Speak softly and carry a big stick; you will go far.

—*Theodore Roosevelt*

I never did a day's work in my life—it was all fun.

—*Thomas Edison*

Every man has his choice of becoming a fountain of joy, or a fountain of sorrow.

Don't just think about your own affairs, but be interested in others, too, and in what they are doing. Your attitude should be the kind that was shown us by Jesus Christ.   —*The Apostle Paul (Philippians 2:4,5)*

One ship drives east and another west,
with the self-same winds that blow;
'tis the set of the sails and not the gales
that determines where they go.
Like the winds of the sea are the ways of fate,
as we voyage along through life;
'tis the set of a soul that decides its goal—
and not the calm or the strife.   *—Ella Wheeler Cox*

It's not the outlook, but the uplook that counts.

The person who always looks down his nose gets
the wrong slant.

Life is a grindstone. But whether it grinds us down or
polishes us up depends on us.   *—L. Thomas Holdcroft*

Circumstances are like a feather bed: comfortable if
you're on top, but smothering if you are underneath.

Character
(also Greatness, Integrity)

Character is never erected on a neglected conscience.

Character is the one thing we make in this world and take with us into the next.

Character is made by many acts; it may be lost by a single act.

Ability will enable a man to get to the top, but it takes character to keep him there.

Reputation and Character
The circumstances amid which you live determine your reputation; the truth you believe determines your character.

Reputation is what you are supposed to be; character is what you are.

Reputation is the photograph; character is the face.

Reputation comes over one from without; character grows up from within.

Reputation is what you have when you come to a new community; character is what you have when you go away.

Your reputation is learned in an hour; your character does not come to light for a year.

Reputation is made in a moment; character is built in a lifetime.

Reputation grows like a mushroom; character grows like the oak.

A single newspaper report gives you your reputation; a life of toil gives you your character.

Reputation makes you rich or makes you poor; character makes you happy or makes you miserable.

Reputation is what men say about you on your tombstone; character is what angels say about you before the throne of God.   —*William Hersey Davis*

The true measure of a man is the height of his ideals, the breadth of his sympathy, the depth of his convictions, and the length of his patience.

Few things are more dangerous to a person's character than having nothing to do and plenty of time in which to do it.

Your reputation can be damaged by the opinions of others. Only you yourself can damage your character.

Faced with crisis, the man of character falls back on himself. He imposes his own stamp of action, takes responsibility for it, makes it his own ... Difficulty attracts the man of character because it is in embracing it that he realizes himself.   —*Charles De Gaulle*

When wealth is lost, nothing is lost;
When health is lost, something is lost;
When character is lost, all is lost.

Talent is nurtured in solitude; character is formed in
the stormy billows of the world.   —*Goethe*

Brains and beauty are nature's gifts; character is your
achievement.

Character is like glass—even a little crack shows.

Take care of your character and your reputation will
take care of itself.

Men of genius are admired; men of wealth are
envied; men of power are feared; but only men of
character are trusted.

Character is a by-product; it is produced in the great
manufacture of daily duty.   —*Woodrow Wilson*

It's what you do when you have nothing to do that
reveals what you are.

The measure of a man's character is not what he
gets from his ancestors, but what he leaves his
descendants.

The two great tests of character are wealth and poverty.

Much may be revealed of a man's character by what excites his laughter.

Your character is what you have left when you've lost everything you can lose.

You don't make your character in a crisis; you exhibit it.
                                        —*Oren Arnold*

People determine your character by observing what you stand for, fall for, and lie for.

Youth and beauty fade; character endures forever.

Have character—don't be one!

A good character is the best tombstone. Those who loved you, and were helped by you, will remember you when forget-me-nots are withered. Carve your name on hearts, and not on marble.
                                        —*Charles Spurgeon*

What you possess in this world will go to someone else when you die, but what you are will be yours forever.

The character of even a child can be known by the
way he acts—whether what he does is pure and right.
                              —*Solomon (Proverbs 20:11)*

Character is much easier kept than recovered.
                                        —*Thomas Paine*

When the late J. P. Morgan was asked what he
considered the best bank collateral, he replied,
"Character!"

How a man plays the game shows something of his
character. How he loses shows all of it.

It is with trifles, and when he is off guard, that a man
best reveals his character.   —*Schopenhauer*

Reputation is what you need to get a job; character is
what you need to keep it.

The measure of a man's character is what he would
do if he knew he would never be found out.
                                        —*Lord Macaulay*

Character is what you really are, reputation is only
what others believe you to be.

Character is what you are in the dark.

The sturdiest tree is not found in the shelter of the forest, but high upon some rocky crag where its daily battle with the elements shapes it into a thing of beauty. So it is with us.

What a man is before God, that he is, and no more.
—*St. Francis of Assisi*

The Lord doesn't take us into deep water to drown us, but to develop us.

It's great to be great, but it's greater to be human.
—*Will Rogers*

Good character, like good soup, is made at home.

Integrity is the basis of all true-blue success.
—*B. C. Forbes*

Be not afraid of greatness: Some are born great, some achieve greatness, and some have greatness thrust upon 'em.
—*William Shakespeare*

You are what you are when no one is around.

Nothing great will ever be achieved without great men, and men are great only if they are determined to be so.
—*Charles De Gaulle*

Greatness lies not in being strong, but in the right use
of strength.   —*Henry W. Beecher*

The Athenian Oath

We will never bring disgrace to this, our nation, by
any act of dishonesty or cowardice, nor ever desert
our suffering comrades in the ranks.

We will fight for the ideals of the nation both alone
and with others.

We will revere and respect our nations's laws, and do
our best to incite a like respect and reverence in those
above us who are prone to annul and set them at
naught.

We will strive unceasingly to quicken the public's
sense of civic duty.

Thus in all these ways we will transmit this nation
not only not less but greater, better, and more beautiful than it was transmitted to us.

The great are great only because we are on our knees.
                                                —*Pierre J. Proudhon*

The greatest danger facing the United States is not
a military lag but a slump in personal and public
integrity.   —*Robert J. McCracken*

A pat on the back develops character—if administered young enough, often enough and low enough.

The integrity of men is to be measured by their conduct, not by their professions.   *—Junius*

Always allow honesty and integrity to increase with your riches.

You cannot drive straight on a twisting lane.
                                               —Russian proverb

Commitment

Commitment is what transforms a promise into
     reality.
It is the words that speak boldly of your intentions.
It is making the time when there is none.
Coming through time after time, year after year after
     year.
Commitment is the stuff character is made of; the
     power to change the face of things.
It is the daily triumph of integrity over skepticism.

Commit your way to the LORD, Trust also in Him,
and He will do it.   —*Psalm 37:5 (NASB)*

Guidance means that I can count on God. Commitment means that God can count on me.

Commitment in the face of conflict produces
character.

For commitment to be meaningful, it must result in
mission.

If I had 300 men who feared nothing but God, hated
nothing but sin, and were determined to know nothing among men but Jesus Christ and Him crucified, I
would set the world on fire.   —*John Wesley*

God does not ask about our ability or our inability,
but about our availability.

It's Not Easy ...
To apologize,
To begin over,
To take advice,
To admit error,
To face a sneer,
To be unselfish,

To be charitable,
To keep on trying,
To be considerate,
To avoid mistakes,
To endure success,
To make a commitment,
To profit by mistakes,
To forgive and forget,
To think and then act,
To stay out of the rut,
To make the best of little,
To control an unruly temper,
To maintain a high standard,
To shoulder a deserved blame,
To recognize the silver lining—
but it always pays.

Commitment is the ability to bind oneself emotionally and intellectually to an idea or task that needs to be completed.

The world has yet to see what God can do with and for and through and in a man who is fully consecrated to Him.　　　　　　　　　　　*—Henry Varley*

It doesn't take such a great man to be a Christian; it just takes all there is of him.　　　　　*—Seth Wilson*

An irate parent phoned her little boy's Sunday school teacher. "Is it true that you told all the kids that they were crazy?" she demanded. "No, I didn't," the teacher replied, "but I did tell them they should all be committed."

The need for devotion to something outside ourselves is even more profound than the need for companionship. If we are not to go to pieces or wither away, we all must have some purpose in life; for no man can live for himself alone.   —*Ross Parmenter*

The quality of a person's life is in direct proportion to his commitment to excellence, regardless of his chosen field of endeavor.   —*Vince Lombardi*

A total commitment is paramount to reaching the ultimate in performance.   —*Tom Flores*

Go thy way, sell whatsoever thou hast, and give to the poor, and thou shalt have treasure in heaven: and come, take up the cross and follow me.
                              —*Jesus (Mark 10:21, KJV)*

Common Sense

Determination to be wise is the first step toward becoming wise! And with your wisdom, develop common sense and good judgement.

—*Solomon (Proverbs 4:7)*

Common sense—a sense more common in its absence than its presence.

Common sense is something everyone can use, yet the only thing not being advertised.

As soon as a man acquires fairly good sense, it is said that he is an old fogy.   —*Ed Howe*

Common sense is very uncommon.   —*Horace Greeley*

Common sense is instinct, and enough of it is genius.
—*H. W. Shaw*

Common sense is not letting your opinions sway your judgment.

Common sense isn't as common as it used to be.
—*Will Rogers*

Common sense is in spite of, not the result of, education.

Men with common sense are admired as counselors; those without it are beaten as servants.
                                        —*Solomon (Proverbs 10:13)*

A little common sense would prevent most divorces—and marriages, too.

Common sense is the knack of seeing things as they are, and doing things as they ought to be done.
                                        —*C. E. Stowe*

One pound of learning requires ten pounds of common sense to apply it.   —*Persian proverb*

It is extremely embarrassing to come to your senses and find out you haven't any.

Man was given five senses: touch, taste, sight, smell and hearing. The successful man has two more: horse and common.

The man who knows right from wrong and has good judgement and common sense is happier than the man who is immensely rich.
                                        —*Solomon (Proverbs 3:13)*

A rabbit's foot is a poor substitute for horse sense.

Common sense in an uncommon degree is what the world calls wisdom. —*S. T. Coleridge*

Horse sense is what keeps a woman from becoming a nag.

A handful of common sense is worth a bushel of learning. —*Spanish proverb*

Success in business is due to administration; and capacity in administration is due to that faculty, power, or quality called common sense.

Nothing astonishes men so much as common sense and plain dealing. —*R. W. Emerson*

The finest education is useless without common sense. —*E. F. Girard*

Good sense: spending less for things you don't need, to impress people you don't like.

Everyone admires a man with good sense, but a man with a warped mind is despised.
—*Solomon (Proverbs 12:8)*

There are forty kinds of lunacy, but only one kind of common sense.

The ideal combination in traffic is to have the horse sense of the driver equal the horsepower of the car.

It takes a lot of horse sense to maintain a stable government.

Emotion makes the world go round, but common sense keeps it from going too fast.

A man with good sense is appreciated. A treacherous man must walk a rocky road.

—Solomon (Proverbs 13:15)

Horse sense vanishes when you begin to feel your oats.

An unusual amount of common sense is sometimes called wisdom.

My son, how I will rejoice if you become a man of common sense. Yes, my heart will thrill to your thoughtful, wise words.

—Solomon (Proverbs 23:15–16)

Confidence

Confidence imparts a wondrous inspiration to its
possessor. —*Milton*

All you need in life is ignorance and confidence, and
then success is sure. —*Mark Twain*

Look backward with gratitude and forward with
confidence.

Confidence is moving on a firm foundation.

It is better to trust the Lord than to put confidence in
men. It is better to take refuge in him than in the
mightiest king! —*Psalm 118:8,9*

Confidence is the feeling you sometimes have before
you fully understand a situation.

In quietness and in confidence shall be your strength.
—*Isaiah (30:15, KJV)*

Did you hear about the cocky and confident man
who did his crossword puzzles with a ballpoint pen?

There is hardly a person who would not struggle to come back if he felt someone had confidence in him and believed he could do it.

And this is the confidence that we have in Him, that, if we ask anything according to His will, He heareth us.   *—John (1 John 5:14, KJV)*

A people without faith in God and themselves cannot survive.

Confidence is keeping your chin up; over-confidence is sticking your neck out.

Skill and confidence are an unconquered army.
                                              —George Herbert

We shall not flag or fail. We shall fight in France, we shall fight on the seas and oceans, we shall fight with growing confidence and growing strength in the air, we shall defend our island, whatever the cost may be, we shall fight on the beaches, we shall fight on the landing grounds, we shall fight in the fields and streets, we shall fight in the hills; we shall never surrender.   *—Sir Winston Churchill*

Confidence is a plant of slow growth.

I can do everything God asks me to with the help of Christ who gives me the strength and power.
> —*The Apostle Paul (Philippians 4:13)*

You must first be a believer if you want to be an achiever.

Confidence is that feeling by which the mind embarks in great and honorable courses with a sure hope and trust in itself.   —*Cicero*

The strength that comes from confidence can be quickly lost in conceit.

He who has lost confidence can lose nothing more.
> —*Boiste*

The line between self-confidence and conceit is very narrow.

Be courteous to all, but intimate with few; and let those few be well tried before you give them your confidence.   —*George Washington*

Mutual confidence is the pillar of friendship.

Confidence and enthusiasm are the great sales producers.   —*Milton*

To whom you tell your secrets, to him you resign
your liberty.   —*Spanish proverb*

Confidence does more to make conversation than
wit.   —*French proverb*

Confidence begets confidence.   —*Latin proverb*

Confidence . . . thrives only on honesty, on honor,
on the sacredness of obligations, on faithful protection and on unselfish performance. Without them it
cannot live.   —*F. D. Roosevelt*

Conscience

Conscience is God's presence in man.
                                —*Emanuel Swedenborg*

A good conscience is a continual Christmas.
                                —*Benjamin Franklin*

Conscience is a device that doesn't keep you from
doing anything; it just keeps you from enjoying it.

A man's conscience is the Lord's searchlight exposing his hidden motives. —*Solomon (Proverbs 20:27)*

Conscience—something that feels terrible when everything else feels wonderful.

Have always a conscience void of offense toward God, and toward men.
—*The Apostle Paul (Acts 24:16, KJV)*

A faithful conscience makes you tell your wife before someone else does.

There is no pillow so soft as a clear conscience.
—*French proverb*

Conscience is a playback of the still small voice that told you not to do it in the first place.

Labor to keep alive in your breast that little spark of celestial fire called conscience. —*George Washington*

Conscience: that still small voice that makes you still smaller.

What the world needs now is an amplifier for the still, small voice.

Many people have their bad memory to thank for their clear conscience.

Conscience is that inner voice that warns us somebody is watching.

Conscience is the root of all true courage; if a man would be brave, let him obey his conscience.
                                          —*J. F. Clarke*

Conscience is that sixth sense that comes to our assistance when we are doing wrong and tells us that we are about to get caught.

The line is often too busy when the conscience wishes to speak.

Quite often when a man thinks his mind is getting broader, it's only his conscience stretching.

A guilty conscience is the mother of invention.
                                          —*Carolyn Wells*

He who has a fight with his conscience and loses, wins.

A man's conscience takes up more room than all the rest of his insides.   —*Huck Finn*

A conscience is what makes you feel guilty for doing
what it wasn't strong enough to keep you from
doing.

There is no hell like a bad conscience.　　*—John Crowne*

Small boy's definition of conscience: Something that
makes you tell your mother before your sister does.

I have lived in all good conscience before God until
this day.　　　　　　*—The Apostle Paul (Acts 23:1, NKJ)*

The conscience is a built-in feature
That haunts the sinner, helps the preacher.
Some sins it makes us turn and run from,
But most it simply takes the fun from.
　　　　　　　　　　　　　　　—Richard Armour

Your conscience is what your mother told you before
you were six months old.　　　　*—Dr. G. B. Chisholm*

The world would be better off if people paid as
much attention to their consciences as they do to
their neighbor's opinions.

Most of us follow our conscience as we follow a
wheelbarrow. We push it in front of us in the direction we want to go.　　　　　　　　*—Billy Graham*

A man has less conscience when in love than in any
other condition.   —*Schopenhauer*

When a man won't listen to his conscience, it's
usually because he doesn't want advice from a
stranger.

Living with a conscience is like driving a car with the
brakes on.   —*Budd Schulberg*

And I know of the future judgment
How dreadful so'er it be
That to sit alone with my conscience
Would be judgment enough for me.
                                           —*Charles Stubbs*

A statesman is a person who takes his ears from the
ground and listens to the still small voice.

The nagging conscience learns to live with the evils it
cannot cure.   —*George Thomson*

Conscience, like a pencil, needs to be sharpened
occasionally.

What better bed than conscience good, to pass the
night in sleep.   —*Thomas Tusser*

The man that loses his conscience has nothing left
that is worth keeping.   *—Isaac Walton*

Conscience gets a lot of credit that belongs to cold
feet.

The best tranquilizer is a good conscience.

Conscience, a terrifying little spite that bat-like winks
by day and wakes by night.   *—John Wolcot*

Conscience is like a baby. It has to go to sleep before
you do.

Conscience helps, but the fear of getting caught
doesn't do any harm either.

Conscience is that small inner voice that tells you the
IRS might check your return.

It is neither safe nor prudent to do anything against
the conscience.   *—Martin Luther*

The testimony of a good conscience is worth more
than a dozen character witnesses.

Conscience is something inside that bothers you
when nothing outside does.

Conscience is that still small voice that yells so loud the morning after.

There is only one way to achieve happiness on this
    terrestrial ball,
And that is to have a clear conscience or none at all.
—Ogden Nash

Cooperation
(also Teamwork, Togetherness)

Apollos and I are working as a team, with the same aim, though each of us will be rewarded for his own hard work. We are only God's co-workers.
—The Apostle Paul (1 Corinthians 3:8)

Cooperation is spelled with two letters: *we.*
—G. M. Verity

Coming together is a beginning; staying together is progress; working together is success.

No one can whistle a symphony. It takes an orchestra to play it.

Partnership is not a principle, but a relationship between persons who share in common enterprise, involving common risks, common privileges, and common responsibilities. Everything depends on the reality of our partnership with one another and each of us with God. —*George Craig Stewart*

A steering committee is a group of four people trying to park a car.

Can two walk together, except they be agreed?
—*Amos (3:3, KJV)*

A lot of people are lonely because they build walls instead of bridges.

If you don't believe in cooperation, look what happens when a car loses one of its wheels.

No man is an island entire to himself. Every man is a piece of the continent, a part of the main. If a clod be washed away by the sea, Europe is the less, as well as if a promontory were, as well as if a manor of thy friends or of thine own were. Any man's death diminishes me, because I am involved in mankind. Therefore never send to know for whom the bell tolls. It tolls for thee. —*John Donne*

Let's remember that it takes both the white and the black keys of the piano to play, "The Star-Spangled Banner."

If civilization is to survive, we must cultivate the science of human relationships—the abilities of all peoples, of all kinds, to live together in the same world at peace.   —*Franklin D. Roosevelt*

You can't applaud with one hand.

There is little chance for people to get together as long as most of us want to be in the front of the bus, the back of the church, and the middle of the road.

Cooperation determines the rate of progress.

If you ever see a turtle on a stump, you know he didn't get there by himself.

Team Spirit: If anything goes bad, I did it. If anything goes semi-good, then we did it. If anything goes real good, then you did it.   —*Bear Bryant*

Cooperation is doing with a smile what you have to do anyway.

One lights the fire, the other fans it.

The village band finished a vigorous and not over-harmonious selection. As the perspiring musicians sank to their seats after acknowledging the applause, the trombonist asked, "What's the next number?"

The leader replied, "The Washington Post March."

"Oh, no," gasped the trombonist. "I just got through playing that!"

Behold, how good and how pleasant it is for brethren to dwell together in unity.   —*Psalm 133:1 (KJV)*

Cooperation will solve many problems. Even freckles would be a nice coat of tan if they would ever get together.

Who passed the ball to you when you scored?

When we think of how no two snowflakes are alike, we find it inspiring that they work so well together on such joint projects as closing schools and making roads impassable.

United we stand, divided we fall.   —*Aesop*

My biggest thrill came the night Elgin Baylor and I combined for 73 points in Madison Square Garden. Elgin had 71 of them.   —*Rod Hundley*

Cooperate! Remember the banana? Every time it leaves the bunch it gets skinned.

The man who pulls on the oars doesn't have time to rock the boat.

If a house be divided against itself, that house cannot stand.   —*Jesus (Mark 3:25, KJV)*

Teamwork is a joint action whose advantage is that there is always someone you can blame if things go wrong.

Liberty and Union, now and forever, one and inseparable.   —*Daniel Webster*

A little boy was playing all alone in the front yard when a neighbor came along and asked where his brother was. "Oh," he said, "he's in the house playing a duet. I finished first."

You've got to have the blocking or you can't gain the yards.   —*Joe Perry*

For there are six things the Lord hates—no, seven: haughtiness, lying, murdering, plotting evil, eagerness to do wrong, a false witness, sowing discord among brothers.   —*Solomon (Proverbs 6:16–19)*

If a moron holds a cow by the ears, a clever man can milk her.

You cannot sink someone else's end of the boat and still keep your own afloat.   —*Charles Brower*

Build for your team a feeling of oneness, of dependence on one another and of strength to be derived by unity.   —*Vince Lombardi*

We fall down by ourselves, but it takes a friendly hand to lift us up.

We must all hang together or assuredly we shall hang separately.   —*Ben Franklin*

When two men in a business always agree, one of them is unnecessary.

A bundle of sticks is always stronger than a single twig.

We may not always see eye to eye, but we should walk hand in hand.

All your strength is in union. All your danger is in discord.   —*Henry W. Longfellow*

Light is the task when many share the toil.   —*Homer*

Courage

Be strong, and let your heart take courage, All you
who hope in the LORD.   —*Psalm 31:24 (NASB)*

This is the way to cultivate courage: First, by standing firm on some conscientious principle, some law
of duty. Next, by being faithful to truth and right on
small occasions and common events. Third, by trust-
ing God for help and power.   —*J. F. Clarke*

He who does not dare will not get his share.

There is nothing in the world so much admired as a
man who knows how to bear unhappiness with
courage.   —*Seneca*

Have courage for the great sorrows of life and
patience for the small ones; and when you have
laboriously accomplished your daily task, go to sleep
in peace. God is awake.   —*Victor Hugo*

There's only a slight difference between keeping
your chin up and sticking your neck out, but it's a
difference worth knowing.

Don't be afraid to take a big step if one is indicated.
You can't cross a chasm in two small jumps.
—*David Lloyd George*

Courage is fear that has said its prayers.

A man's courage can sustain his broken body, but
when courage dies, what hope is left?
—*Solomon (Proverbs 18:14)*

A man of courage is also full of faith. —*Cicero*

When there is no money, half is gone; when there is
no courage, all is gone.

Wine gives false courage; hard liquor leads to brawls;
what fools men are to let it master them, making
them reel drunkenly down the street!
—*Solomon (Proverbs 20:1)*

Don't consult a coward about war.

You'd be surprised how often nerve succeeds.

Lord, grant me the serenity to accept the things I
cannot change, the courage to change the things
I can, and the wisdom to know the difference.
—*St. Francis of Assisi*

The wishbone will never replace the backbone.
—*Will Henry*

The test of tolerance comes when we are in the majority; the test of courage comes when we are in a minority.   —*Ralph Sockman*

Don't be afraid to go out on a limb—that's where the fruit is!

He who lacks courage thinks with his legs.

One man with courage makes a majority.
—*Andrew Jackson*

It's courage and character that make the difference between players and great players, between great surgeons and ones who bury their mistakes.
—*Coach Pete Carrol*

So what if they're taller? We'll play big!
—*Coach George Ireland*

Success is never final. Failure is never fatal. It's courage that counts.   —*Coach John Wooden*

So lead on with courage and strength!
—*Israelites to Joshua (Joshua 1:18)*

When moral courage feels that it is in the right, there is no personal daring of which it is incapable.
—*Leigh Hunt*

Be strong! Be courageous! Do not be afraid of them! For the Lord your God will be with you. He will neither fail you nor forsake you.
—*Moses (Deuteronomy 31:6)*

It is easy to be brave from a safe distance.   —*Aesop*

Courage is the quality of mind that makes us forget how afraid we are.

Courage is the first of human qualities because it is the quality which guarantees all others.
—*Winston Churchill*

No one wants to be brave anymore—just chief!

Courage isn't a brilliant dash,
A daring deed in a moment's flash;
It isn't an instantaneous thing
Born of despair with a sudden spring.
But it's something deep in the soul of man
That is working always to serve some plan.
—*Edgar A. Guest*

Keep your fears to yourself, but share your courage
with others.   —*Robert Louis Stevenson*

Behold the turtle. He makes progress only when he
sticks his neck out.   —*James B. Conant*

Creativity
(also Ideas)

Happiness lies in the joy of achievement and the
thrill of creative effort.   —*Franklin D. Roosevelt*

When a child asks difficult questions, invention is the
necessity of Mother.

Never tell people *how* to do things. Tell them what to
do and they will surprise you with their ingenuity.
                                    —*George S. Patton, Jr.*

Another war worth waging is one against the
poverty of ideas.

The mind once stretched by a great idea can never
return to its original dimensions.

God gives the nuts, but He does not crack them.

The best way to put an idea across is to wrap it up in a person.

The trouble with a public address system is that it amplifies a speaker's voice, but not his ideas.
—*Martha J. Beckman*

Getting a new idea should be like sitting on a tack; it should make you get up and do something about it.

Test new ideas; keep the old for emergencies.

Louis Pasteur had nothing to work with but the germ of an idea.

The reason ideas die quickly in some people's heads is that they can't stand solitary confinement.

Don't just entertain new ideas—put them to work!

If the paper clip were invented today, it probably would have ten moving parts, five transistors and require a service man three times a year.

When man learned that he could not live by bread alone, he invented the sandwich.   —*Bob Barnes*

The fellow who invented the life-saver really made a
mint.   —*Gordon Yardy*

New ideas hurt some minds the same as new shoes
hurt some feet.

Creativity isn't necessary if you always have the ball.

What America really needs most are those things
that money cannot buy.

Good teachers light up lives with creative ideas, illu-
mine minds with joyful enthusiasm, and brighten
futures with inspired encouragement.
                                         —*William A. Ward*

Nothing dies quicker than a new idea in a closed
mind.

Unexpressed ideas are of no more value than kernels
in a nut before it has been cracked.

An idea is a funny little thing that won't work unless
you do.

A new idea is delicate. It can be killed by a sneer or a
yawn, stabbed to death by a quip or worried to
death by a frown.

Good ideas need landing gear as well as wings.
—*C. D. Jackson*

How good a red-hot idea is depends on how much heat it loses when somebody throws cold water on it.

A good idea is one that hits the other fellow with a bolt of envy.

The wheel was man's greatest invention until he got behind it.

The man who invented the eraser had the human race pretty well sized up.

Nothing can revive an idea whose time has passed.
—*E. L. C. Broomes*

The important thing is not to stop questioning. Curiosity has its own reason for existing. One cannot help but be in awe when he contemplates the mysteries of eternity, of life, of the marvelous structure of reality. It is enough if one tries merely to comprehend a little of this mystery every day. Never lose a holy curiosity.   —*Albert Einstein*

Do not follow where the path may lead. Go instead where there is no path, and leave a trail.

"OOPS"

An irate banker
demanded that
Alex Graham Bell
remove "that toy"
from his office.
That toy was
the telephone.

A Hollywood producer
scrawled a curt
rejection note on
a manuscript that became
"Gone With the Wind."

Henry Ford's largest
original investor
sold all his stock in 1906.

Roebuck sold out to Sears
for $25,000 in 1895.
Today Sears may sell
$25,000 worth of goods
in 16 seconds.

The next time someone offers you an idea that leaves
you cold, put it on the back burner and let it warm up.

An inventor is a crack-pot who becomes a genius
when his idea catches on.

There is one thing stronger than all the armies in the world, and that is an idea whose time has come.

—Victor Hugo

Criticism

He has the right to criticize who has the heart to help.

—Abraham Lincoln

Three Gates

If you are tempted to reveal
A tale to you someone has told
About another, make it pass,
Before you speak, three gates of gold.

These narrow gates: First, "Is it true?"
Then, "Is it needful?" In your mind
Give truthful answer. And the next
Is last and narrowest, "Is it kind?"

And if to reach your lips at last
It passes through these gateways three,
Then you may tell the tale, nor fear
What the result of speech may be.

—From The Arabian

The question is not what a man can scorn, or dis-
parage, or find fault with, but what he can love, and
value, and appreciate.   —*John Ruskin*

Don't criticize and speak evil about each other, dear
brothers. If you do, you will be fighting against
God's law of loving one another, declaring it is
wrong. But your job is not to decide whether this
law is right or wrong, but to obey it.   —*James (4:11)*

Critics are people who go places and boo things.

He who throws dirt loses ground.

Bernard Baruch once reminded us that two things are
hard on the heart—running up stairs and running
down people.

Criticism should not be querulous and wasting, all
knife and root-pulling, but guiding, instructive, inspiring—a south wind and not an east wind.
                           —*Ralph Waldo Emerson*

He who cannot stand the heat should stay out of the
kitchen.

Have you ever noticed that most of the knocking is
done by folks who don't know how to ring the bells?

If you refuse criticism you will end in poverty and
disgrace; if you accept criticism your are on the road
to fame.   —*Solomon (Proverbs 13:18)*

If criticism comes to say
Some unthoughtful word today
That may drive a friend away,
Don't say it!

If you've heard a word of blame
Cast upon your neighbor's name
That may injure his fair fame,
Don't tell it!

If malicious gossip's tongue
Some vile slander may have flung
On the old or young,
Don't repeat it!

Thoughtful, kind, helpful speech,
Is a gift promised to each—
This is the lesson it would teach:
Don't abuse it!

If you profit from constructive criticism you will be
elected to the wise man's hall of fame. But to reject
criticism is to harm yourself and your own best
interests.   —*Solomon (Proverbs 15:31,32)*

Don't refuse to accept criticism; get all the help you
can.   —*Solomon (Proverbs 23:12)*

Handling criticism: If it's untrue, disregard it; if it's
unfair, keep from irritation; if it's ignorant, smile; if
it's justified, learn from it.

Death
(also Living)

Don't look to men for help; their greatest leaders fail;
for every man must die. His breathing stops, life
ends, and in a moment all he planned for himself is
ended.   —*Psalm 146:3,4*

Ambition and death are alike in this: Neither is ever
satisfied.   —*Solomon (Proverbs 27:20)*

We are but tenants, and . . . shortly the great Land-
lord will give us notice that our lease has expired.
                                      —*Joseph Jefferson*

Death—a path that must be trod, if man would ever
pass to God.   —*Thomas Parnell*

Let Me Die, Working
Let me die, working.
Still tackling plans unfinished, tasks undone!
Clean to its end, swift may my race be run.
No laggard steps, no faltering, no shirking;
Let me die, working!

Let me die, thinking.
Let me fare forth still with an open mind,
Fresh secrets to unfold, new truths to find,
My soul undimmed, alert, no questions blinking;
Let me die, thinking!

Let me die, laughing.
No sighing o'er past sins; they are forgiven.
Spilled on this earth are all the joys of Heaven;
The wine of life, the cup of mirth quaffing.
Let me die, laughing!   —*S. Hall Young*

Death—the poor man's doctor.   —*German proverb*

Death—the inevitable hour.   —*Thomas Gray*

Did you hear about the undertaker who closed his letters with the words, "Eventually yours"?

The man who strays from common sense will end up dead!   —*Solomon (Proverbs 21:16)*

Before every man there lies a wide and pleasant road
he thinks is right, but it ends in death.
                              —*Solomon (Proverbs 16:25)*

Death—a punishment to some, to some a gift, and to
many a favor.   —*Seneca*

I know of nobody who has a mind to die this year.
                              —*William Shakespeare*

Death—the great equalizer of mankind.

God made death so we'd know when to stop.
                              —*Steven Stiles*

That death is as sure as taxes
Has received wide recognition,
But death has this advantage—
It's a one-time proposition.

Death—the terror of the rich, the desire of the poor.
                              —*Joseph Zabara*

It is destined that men die only once, and after that
comes judgement.   —*The Apostle Paul (Hebrews 9:27)*

It is important that when we come to die we have
nothing to do but to die.   —*Charles Hodge*

The hardest thing of all—to die rightly—an exam
nobody is spared—and how many pass it?
                                        —Dag Hammarskjold

When an evil man dies, his hopes all perish, for they
are based on this earthly life.
                                        —Solomon (Proverbs 11:7)

If I can get a man to think seriously about death for
five minutes, I can get him saved.   *—Dwight L. Moody*

A lot of people die at 40 but are not buried until 30
years later.   *—George Patton, Jr.*

It's not up to you to choose how you're going to die,
but it is up to you to choose how you're going to live.

I've never had guilt at all. Things happen for a reason.
The thing it taught me is that you have no control
over your life. It's in God's hands.
                    *—Reba McEntire, following the deaths of
                    seven band members and her tour man-
                    ager in a plane crash, March 16, 1991*

The whole city celebrates a good man's success—and
also the godless man's death.
                                        —Solomon (Proverbs 11:10)

Ninety-five percent of the people who die today had expected to live a lot longer.   —*Albert M. Wells, Jr.*

So live that when death comes the mourners will outnumber the cheering section.

There are three important steps to take in preparation for a holy death. And these three principles should be practiced throughout life. (1) Expect that death will come knocking at your gates at any time; this will keep your priorities straight. (2) Value your time, for it is the most precious possession you have. (3) Refrain from a soft and easy life; stress the holy life of self-discipline, labor and alertness. Engage each day in self-examination.   —*Jeremy Taylor*

A Southern preacher's comment at the funeral, "The shell's here, but the nut's gone."

Death is not a period but a comma in the story of life.

At the end of life we shall not be asked how much pleasure we had in it, but how much service we gave in it; not how full it was of success, but how full it was of sacrifice; not how happy we were; not how ambition was gratified, but how love served.
                                             —*Hugh Black*

The path of the godly leads to life. So, why fear
death?   *—Solomon (Proverbs 12:28)*

The saddest thing from birth to sod
Is a dying man who has no God.

The good man finds life; the evil man, death.
                                —Solomon (Proverbs 11:19)

Secretary's dilemma, "Since I've used all my sick days
. . . I'm calling in dead!"

Life Begins At Seventy
Psalm 90:10: "Threescore years and ten."

Between the ages of 70 and 83 Commodore Vander-
bilt added about $100 million to his fortune.

Kant at 74 wrote his *Anthropology, Metaphysics of
Ethics,* and *Strife of the Faculties.*

Tintoretto at 74 painted the vast *Paradise,* a canvas
74 feet by 30 feet.

Verdi at 74 produced his masterpiece, *Othello;* at 80,
Falstaff; and at 85, the famous *Ave Maria, Stabet
Mater,* and *Te Deum.*

Lamarck at 78 completed his great zoological work,
The Natural History of the Invertebrates.

Oliver Wendell Holmes at 79 wrote *Over the Teacups.*

Cato at 80 began the study of Greek.

Goethe at 80 completed *Faust.*

Tennyson at 83 wrote "Crossing the Bar."

Titian at 98 painted his historic picture of the Battle
of Lepanto.   —*The Golden Book*

Decision-Making

Somewhere along the line of our development we
discover what we really are, and then we make our
decision for which we are responsible. Make that
decision primarily for yourself because you can never
really live anyone else's life.   —*Eleanor Roosevelt*

We should make our plans—counting on God to
direct us.   —*Solomon (Proverbs 16:9)*

Never make a decision based on fear.

There is a time when we must firmly choose the
course we will follow, or the relentless drift of events
will make the decision.   —*Herbert V. Prochnow*

The reason most people change their minds is that they never find one worth keeping.

We toss the coin, but it is the Lord who controls its decision   —*Solomon (Proverbs 16:33)*

One of the hardest decisions in life is when to start middle age.

One of life's difficult decisions is picking the super-market check-out line that will move fastest.

He who insists on seeing with perfect clearness before he decides never decides.
                          —*Henri Frederic Amiel*

Almost everyone knows the difference between right and wrong, but some just hate to make decisions.
                          —*Joseph Salak*

Sign at the crossroads in a Southwestern desert state: "Be careful which road you take—you'll be on it for the next 200 miles."

The answer is maybe—and that's final!

No one learns to make right decisions without being free to make wrong ones.

"I see what's wrong," whispered the referee to himself, as threats and nasty remarks were coming from every direction for his last decision. "The ref should be stationed in the grandstand."

What a shame—yes, how stupid!—to decide before knowing the facts!   —*Solomon (Proverbs 18:13)*

In every success story, you find someone has made a courageous decision.   —*Peter F. Drucker*

Making a decision, even a bad one, is better than making no decision at all.   —*Jesse Aweida*

If I had to sum up what constitutes a good manager in one word, I would say that everything depends on decisions. And a good decision can turn into a bad one if it is applied too late.   —*Lee Iacocca*

Your capacity to say "No" determines your capacity to say "Yes" to greater things.   —*E. Stanley Jones*

We make our decisions, and then our decisions turn around and make us.   —*F. W. Boreham*

If you would achieve your goals and be a successful, dynamic person, then your very first step must be to make up your mind.   —*Alfred Montapert*

A wise man makes his own decisions, an ignorant man follows the public opinion.   —*Chinese proverb*

Look at it, size it up, but don't "postpone your life" just because you can't make up your mind.
                              —*Omar Bradley*

Decision and perseverance are the noblest qualities of man.   —*Goethe*

New automobiles come equipped with a right-turn and left-turn signal. What we need is one more to indicate "undecided."

Choose you this day whom you will serve.
                              —*Joshua (24:15, KJV)*

Decision—what an executive is forced to make when he can't get anyone to serve on a committee.

No wind serves him who addresses his voyage to no certain port.   —*Montaigne*

One of these days is none of these days.
                              —*English proverb*

A double-minded man is unstable in all his ways.
                              —*James (1:8, KJV)*

God gives the nuts, but He does not crack them.

Procrastination is the art of keeping up with yesterday.   —*Don Marquis*

All heaven's glory is within and so is hell's fierce
burning. You must yourself decide in which direction
you are turning.   —*Angelus Silesius*

Patience may be simply the inability to make a
decision.

The man who has not learned to say no will be a
weak if not a wretched man as long as he lives.

Decision is a sharp knife that cuts clean and straight;
indecision is a dull one that hacks and tears and
leaves ragged edges behind it.   —*Gordon Graham*

Before you start looking for a peg, decide what hole
you want to fill.

Making decisions is simple: get the facts; seek God's
guidance; form a judgement; act on it; worry no more.
                                          —*Charles E. Bennett*

Once the facts are clear, the decisions jump at you.
                                          —*Peter Drucker*

A man should give a lot of thought to a sudden decision.

Not to decide is to decide.   *—Harvey Cox*

An executive is a guy who can take as long as he wants to make a snap decision.

Determination

Nothing is so common as unsuccessful men with talent. They lack only determination.
          —Charles Swindoll

I am only one, but I am one. I cannot do everything but I can do something; and what I can do, that I ought to do; and what I ought to do, by the grace of God I shall do.   *—Edward Everett Hale*

No person in the world has more determination than he who can stop after eating one peanut.

Some men succeed because they are destined to, but most men because they are determined to.

The difference between a successful person and
others is not a lack of strength, not a lack of
knowledge, but rather a lack of will.

—*Vince Lombardi*

The difference between the impossible and the
possible lies in a man's determination.

—*Tommy Lasorda*

In a race, everyone runs but only one person gets first
prize. So run your race to win.

—*The Apostle Paul (1 Corinthians 9:24)*

A dead fish can float downstream, but it takes a live
fish to swim upstream.

He who doesn't climb the mountain cannot see the
view.

If Christopher Columbus had turned back, no one
would have blamed him. No one would have remem-
bered him either.

We don't fully realize the hardships of our pioneer
ancestors until we remember that, day after day,
they plodded their way westward into the setting
sun—without sunglasses.

Consider the hammer:
It keeps its head.
It doesn't fly off the handle.
It keeps pounding away.
It finds the point then drives it home.
It looks at the other side, too, and thus clinches the
    matter.
It makes mistakes, but when it does, it starts all over.
It is the only knocker in the world that does any
    good.

Determination to be wise is the first step toward
becoming wise!   —*Solomon (Proverbs 4:7)*

If you don't stand for something, you'll fall for
anything.

Personnel manager to applicant: What we're after is a
man of vision; a man with drive, determination, fire;
a man who never quits; a man who can inspire
others; a man who can pull the company's bowling
team out of last place!

Quality is never an accident; it is always the result of
high intention, determined effort, intelligent direction
and skilled execution; it represents the wise choice of
many alternatives.

Curious people ask questions; determined people find answers.

Big shots are only little shots who kept on shooting.
—*Dale Carnegie*

Quitters in the church are like motors—they sputter before they miss and miss before they quit.

Discipline

Discipline is the soul of an army. It makes small numbers formidable, procures success to the weak, and esteem to all.   —*George Washington*

Discipline is the refining fire by which talent becomes ability.

The undisciplined is a headache to himself and a heartache to others, and is unprepared to face the stern realities of life.

A stern discipline pervades all nature, which is a little cruel that it may be very kind.   —*Spenser*

He who requires much from himself and little from others will keep himself from being the object of resentment. —*Confucius*

Life is always a discipline, for the lower animals as well as for men; it is so dangerous that only by submitting to some sort of discipline can we become equipped to live in any true sense at all.
—*Havelock Ellis*

Do not consider painful what is good for you.
—*Euripides*

If you refuse to discipline your son, it proves you don't love him; for if you love him you will be prompt to punish him. —*Solomon (Proverbs 13:24)*

No pain, no palm; no thorns, no throne; no gall, no glory; no cross, no crown. —*Penn*

The study of God's Word, for the purpose of discovering God's will, is the secret discipline which has formed the greatest characters.
—*James W. Alexander*

No man is free who cannot command himself.
—*Pythagoras*

Character is, by its very nature, the product of proba-
tionary discipline.   —*Austin Phelps*

The cure of crime is not in the *electric* chair, but in the
high chair.

A man in old age is like a sword in a shop window
... Men that look upon the perfect blade do not
imagine the process by which it was completed ...
Man is a sword; daily life is the workshop; and God
is the artificer; and those cares which beat upon the
anvil, and file the edge, and eat in, acid-like, the
inscription on the hilt—those are the very things that
fashion the man.   —*H. W. Beecher*

One reason for juvenile delinquency—parents don't
burn their kids' britches behind them.

A pat on the back develops character—if administered young enough, often enough, and low enough.

If you refuse to discipline your son, it proves you
don't love him; for if you love him you will be
prompt to punish him.   —*Solomon (Proverbs 13:24)*

People who are always walking on clouds leave too
many things up in the air.

Storms make oaks take deeper root.
—*George Santayana*

The sturdiest tree is not found in the shelter of the forest, but high upon some rocky crag where its daily battle with the elements shapes it into a thing of beauty. So it is with your children.

Discipline, once considered "standard household equipment," has fallen on hard times, and in its place permissiveness reigns.

To live a disciplined life, and to accept the result of that discipline as the will of God—that is the mark of the man.   —*Tom Landry*

Discipline is demanded of the athlete to win a game. Discipline is required for the captain running his ship. Discipline is needed for the pianist to practice for the concert. Only in the matter of personal conduct is the need for discipline questioned. But if parents believe standards are necessary, then discipline certainly is needed to attain them.

Dreams
(see also Future)

The Dream
Ah, great it is to believe the dream
As we stand in youth by the starry stream;
But a greater thing is to fight life through,
And at the end, "The dream is true!"

—*Edwin Markham*

Reach high, for stars lie hidden in your soul.
Dream deep, for every dream precedes the goal.

—*Pamela Vaull Starr*

Credo
I believe in America:
because in it we are free—free to choose our govern-
    ment, to speak our minds, to observe our differ-
    ent religions;
because we are generous with our freedom—we
    share our rights with those who disagree with us;
because we hate no people and covet no people's
    land;
because we are blessed with a natural and varied
    abundance;

because we set no limit to a man's achievement—in
    mine, factory, field, or service in business or the
    arts—an able man, regardless of class or creed,
    can realize his ambition;
because we have great dreams—and because we
    have the opportunity to make those dreams
    come true.   *—Wendell L. Willkie*

Some men see things as they are and say, "Why?" I
dream things that never were and say, "Why not?"
                              —George Bernard Shaw

Impossible Dreams
Everyone with the faintest ambition for fame
Has what seems an impossible dream,
That someday a big marquee will emblazon his name,
Or bold headlines enhance his esteem.

All our great inventors, composers and such,
The creator of things quite extreme,
Didn't start their ideas with a magical touch,
Just their hope of a possible scheme.

They all had the gut instinct to give it a fling,
And endeavored to see the dream through,
And proved to the world that there is such a thing
As impossible dreams that come true.
                              —Dave Wadley

Some people who think they are dreamers are just sleepers.

The poorest of all men is not the man without a cent but the man without a dream.

To dream anything that you want to dream—that is the beauty of the human mind. To do anything you want to do—that is the strength of the human will. To trust yourself to test your limits—that is the courage to succeed.   —*Bernard Edmonds*

God . . . is able to do far more than we would dare to ask or even dream of—infinitely beyond our highest prayers, desires, thoughts or hopes.
                    —*The Apostle Paul (Ephesians 3:20)*

I saw a man chasing the horizon. I shouted to him, "You'll never reach it."
He replied, "You lie," and rushed on.

Castles in the air are nice until you step out the door. They are all right until you try to move into them.

Did you hear about the man who dreamed he ate a five-pound marshmallow? When he woke up his pillow was gone.

It doesn't do any harm to dream, providing you get up and hustle when the alarm goes off.

You can never make your dreams come true by oversleeping.

Daydreaming: wishcraft.   —*Bert Murray*

We create our tomorrows by what we dream today.

All big men are dreamers. They see things in the soft haze of a spring day or in the red fire of a long winter's evening. Some of us let our dreams die, but others nourish them and protect them, nurse them through bad days till they bring them to sunshine and light which always comes to those who sincerely believe that their dreams will come true.

—*Woodrow Wilson*

Endurance
(also Fortitude, Tenacity, Strength, Bravery)

Endurance test: entertaining a pest who says nothing, or listening to a bore who does all the talking.

Fortitude: the courage with which some people go through life bearing the misfortunes of others.

Tenacity: the perseverance that results from a strong will, or the obstinacy that results from a strong won't.

The LORD is the everlasting God, the Creator of the ends of the earth. He does not faint or grow weary, his understanding is unsearchable. He gives power to the faint, and to him who has no might he increases strength.   —*Isaiah (40:28,29, RSV)*

And ah, for a man to arise in me,
That the man I am may cease to be!
                         —*Alfred, Lord Tennyson*

When you have no choice, at least be brave.

The first and final thing you have to do in this world is to last in it and not be smashed by it, and it is the same way with your work. This is at once a rule for the conduct of life and a rule for the conduct of art: to last, and to do work that will last.
                         —*Ernest Hemingway*

True fortitude is seen in great exploits that justice warrants and that wisdom guides.   —*Joseph Addison*

God could have kept Daniel out of the lion's den. He could have kept Paul and Silas out of jail. He could have kept the three Hebrew children out of the fiery furnace. But God has never promised to keep us out of hard places. What He has promised is to go with us through every hard place, and to bring us through victoriously.

Enjoy what you can; and endure what you must.

—*Goethe*

Fortitude is victory. —*Oliver Goldsmith*

Fortitude is the marshal of thought, the armor of the will, and the fort of reason. —*Francis Bacon*

Thank God for the iron in the blood of our fathers.

—*Theodore Roosevelt*

Fortitude and the power of fixing attention are the two marks of a great mind.

Facing it—always facing it—that's the way to get through. Face it! That's enough for any man.

—*Joseph Conrad*

Strength comes from struggle; weakness from ease.

—*B. C. Forbes*

He that endureth to the end shall be saved.
                              —*Matthew (10:22, KJV)*

God will lead you to no waters He cannot part, no brink He cannot cross, no pain He cannot bear.

Endurance is patience concentrated.   —*Carlyle*

Lord, give me the tenacity and determination of a weed.

George Washington fought nine major battles in the Revolutionary War. He lost six of these battles but won the war.

Be like a postage stamp, stick to one thing until you get there.   —*Josh Billings*

Today's mighty oak is just yesterday's nut that held its ground.

And let us not get tired of doing what is right, for after a while we will reap a harvest of blessing if we don't get discouraged and give up.
                    —*The Apostle Paul (Galatians 6:9)*

Our strength often increases in proportion to the obstacles imposed upon it.   —*Paul de Rapin*

A diamond is a piece of coal that stuck to its job.

He conquers who endures. —*Persius*

The first thing a child should learn is how to endure.
It is what he will have most to know.
—*Jean-Jacques Rousseau*

A handicap does not mean permanent prohibition
from fame, fortune and fulfillment. Milton and
Homer were blind. Beethoven probably never heard
his last symphonies as deafness closed in on him.
Franklin Roosevelt was a four-term president in a
wheelchair.

What cannot be cured must be endured.

Fortitude—in itself an essential virtue—is a guard to
every other virtue. —*John Locke*

The man who cannot survive bad times will not see
good times.

If you carry your own lantern, you will endure the
dark.

Endurance is the crowning quality, and patience all
the passion of great hearts. —*James Russell Lowell*

'Tis a lesson you should heed,
Try, try again.
If at first you don't succeed,
Try, try again.   —*William E. Hickson*

When you get into a tight place and everything goes
against you, till it seems as though you could not
hold on a minute longer, never give up then, for that
is just the place and time that the tide will turn.
                              —*Harriet Beecher Stowe*

Excellence

Excellence can be obtained if you . . .
    care more than others think is wise;
    risk more than others think is safe;
    dream more than others think is practical;
    expect more than others think is possible.

Excellence is to do a common thing in an uncommon
way.   —*Booker T. Washington*

Excellence is never granted to man but as the reward
of labor.   —*Sir Joshua Reynolds*

The pursuit of excellence is gratifying and healthy.
The pursuit of perfection is frustrating, neurotic and a
terrible waste of time.   —*Edwin Bliss*

The society which scorns excellence in plumbing
because plumbing is a humble activity and tolerates
shoddiness in philosophy because it is an exalted
activity will have neither good plumbing nor good
philosophy. Neither its pipes nor its theories will
hold water.

One that desires to excel should endeavor it in those
things that are in themselves most excellent.
                                         —*Epictetus*

Those who attain to any excellence commonly spend
life in some one single pursuit, for excellence is not
often gained upon easier terms.   —*Johnson*

Every job is a self-portrait of the person who did it.
Autograph your work with excellence.

The difference between ordinary and extra-ordinary
is that little extra.

We are what we repeatedly do. Excellence then is
not an act but a habit.

The quality of a person's life is in direct proportion to that person's commitment to excellence, regardless of the chosen field of endeavor.   —*Vince Lombardi*

Excellence resides in quality not in quantity. The best is always few and rare; much lowers value.
                                                  —*Gracian*

We measure the excellency of other men by some excellency we conceive to be in ourselves.
                                              —*John Selden*

Excellent things are rare.   —*Plato*

The secret of joy is contained in one word—excellence. To know how to do something well is to enjoy it.   —*Pearl Buck*

Desire is the key to motivation, but it's the determination and commitment to an unrelenting pursuit of your goal—a commitment to excellence—that will enable you to attain the success you seek.
                                            —*Mario Andretti*

Excellence is not a matter of chance, it's a matter of choice.

Human excellence means nothing
Unless it works with the consent of God.   —*Euripides*

Experience

I have but one lamp by which my feet are guided,
and that is the lamp of experience.   —*Patrick Henry*

Experience is what you have left when everything
else is gone.

Experience is a wonderful thing. It enables you to
recognize a mistake when you make it again.

The taste of defeat has a richness of experience all its
own.   —*Bill Bradley*

Experience is the blind man's dog.

Read the history books and see—for we were born
but yesterday and know so little; our days here on
earth are as transient as shadows. But the wisdom of
the past will teach you. The experience of others will
speak to you.   —*Bildad to Job (Job 8:8–10)*

Experience is a demanding teacher—no graduates, no degrees, some survivors.

Experience should be a guidepost and not a hitching post.

Listen to the voice of experience, but also make use of your brains.

Good judgement comes from experience. Experience comes from bad judgement.   —*Mark Twain*

Some people learn from their experiences; some never recover from them.

Burned children spurn the fire.

A wise man learns by the experiences of others. An ordinary man learns by his own experience. A fool learns by nobody's experience.

Once bitten, twice shy.

Experience is a hard teacher because she gives the test first, the lesson afterwards.   —*Vernon Law*

When down in the mouth remember Jonah—he came out all right.   —*Thomas Edison*

Experience may be the best teacher but the one I had in grammar school was much prettier.

—*Don McNeill*

There are no vacations from the school of experience.

Don't, like the cat, try to get more out of an experience than there is in it. The cat, having sat upon a hot stove lid, will not sit upon a hot stove lid again. Nor upon a cold stove lid.   —*Mark Twain*

There is only one thing more painful than learning from experience, and that is *not* learning from experience.

Experience—something we would all be glad to sell for less than we paid for it.

The glory of young men is their strength; of old men, their experience.   —*Solomon (Proverbs 20:29)*

Experience is the school that repeats the instruction if you flunk it the first time.

One thorn of experience is worth a whole wilderness of warning.

Experience is yesterday's answer to today's problem.

Every time you graduate from the school of experience someone thinks up a new course.

A new broom sweeps clean, but an old one knows where the dirt is.

If you could sell your experience for what it cost, you would never need social security.   —*Ben Bergor*

There's no fool like an old fool—you just can't beat experience.

Experience is the best method of acquiring knowledge, except when learning about mushrooms and toadstools.

Those who cannot remember the past are condemned to repeat it.

Experience is compulsory education.

Experience is not what happens to you, it is what you do with what happens to you.   —*Aldous Huxley*

I have been young and now I am old. And in all my years I have never seen the Lord forsake a man who loves him; nor have I seen the children of the godly go hungry.   —*David (Psalm 37:25)*

Facts

A rebel doesn't care about the facts. All he wants to
do is yell.   —*Solomon (Proverbs 18:2)*

Facts do not cease to exist because they are ignored.
                                          —*Aldous Huxley*

The people when given the facts will never make a
mistake.   —*Thomas Jefferson*

Facts, when combined with ideas, constitute the
greatest force in the world.

Every man has a right to his opinion, but no man has
a right to be wrong in his facts.   —*Bernard Baruch*

I grow daily to honor facts more and more and
theory less and less.   —*Thomas Carlyle*

The wise man looks ahead. The fool attempts to fool
himself and won't face facts.
                                          —*Solomon (Proverbs 14:8)*

Digging for facts is better mental exercise than jumping to conclusions.

Get the facts at any price, and hold on tightly to all
the good sense you can get.
                              —*Solomon (Proverbs 23:23)*

The hardest thing about facts is facing them.

A hardliner's admission: "My mind's made up! Don't
confuse me with the facts!"

I would have you learn this great fact: that a life of
doing things right is the wisest life there is.
                              —*Solomon (Proverbs 4:11)*

We wouldn't call him a liar. Let's just say that he
lives on the wrong side of the facts.

The highest art of professional management requires
the ability to literally "smell" a real fact from all
others—and moreover to have the temerity, intellectual curiosity, guts and/or plain politeness, if necessary, to be sure what you have is indeed what we
call an "unshakable fact."   —*Harold Geneen*

Get your facts first, then you can distort 'em as you
please.   —*Mark Twain*

Facts are stubborn things.   —*Tobias Smollett*

When you shoot an arrow of truth, dip its point in
honey.   —*Arab proverb*

The chief value of the new fact is to enhance the
great and constant fact of life.   —*Emerson*

Any fact is better established by two or three good
testimonies, than by a thousand arguments.

A sure way to stop a red-hot argument is to lay a few
cold facts on it.

[Wisdom] cries, "How long will you go on being
fools? How long will you scoff at wisdom and fight
the facts?"   —*Solomon (Proverbs 1:22)*

Fact is fact and feeling is feeling; never does the
second change the first.

When you have duly arrayed your "facts" in logical
order, lo, it is like an oil lamp that you have made,
filled and trimmed, but which sheds no light unless
first you light it.   —*Saint-Exupéry*

Failure
(also Defeats, Winners, Losers)

It is defeat that turns bone to flint, gristle to muscle, and makes men valuable as it forms those heroic natures that have made the world a better place. Often victory slips through the door of defeat unnoticed.

Defeat never comes to any man until he admits it.
—*Joseph Daniels*

Show me a man who is a good loser and I'll show you a man who is playing golf with his boss.

After resigning as coach of the Iowa State women's basketball team, which finished the season with four-teen straight defeats, Lynn Wheeler remarked: "I've taken this team as far as I can."

He who procrastinates struggles with failure and lack of fulfillment.

Many of life's failures are men who did not realize how close they were to success when they gave up.

Most men fail, not through lack of education, but from lack of dogged determination, from lack of dauntless will.

Restlessness is discontent—and discontent is the first necessity of progress. Show me a thoroughly satisfied man, and I will show you a failure.
—*Thomas Edison*

Pride goes before destruction and haughtiness before a fall. —*Solomon (Proverbs 16:18)*

He who leaves home to set the world on fire often comes back for more matches.

The only something you get for nothing is failure.

A college freshman sent home a telegram saying, "Mom! Have failed everything, prepare Pop!"
The reply came the next day, "Pop prepared . . . prepare yourself!"

Success comes in cans; failure comes in can'ts.

The road to success is always under construction. Winning isn't everything, but wanting to win is.
—*Arnold Palmer*

Winners find ways to make things work. Losers find excuses why things don't work.

Defeat isn't bitter if you don't swallow it.

A few years ago, Montana State University had a bad football season, but the coach faced the new year optimistically. "We're sure to improve," he said. "We lost all ten games last year. This year we have only nine scheduled."

Falling down doesn't make you a failure, but staying down does.

Failure is a better teacher than success, but she seldom finds an apple on her desk.

God gave us two ends—one to sit on and one to think with. A person's success or failure depends on the one he uses most.

Failure is not necessarily missing the target, but aiming too low.

I always turn to the sports page first. The sports page records people's accomplishments; the front page nothing but man's failures.

—*Supreme Court Justice Earl Warren*

Don't hug your defeats. Analyze your victories.

"How did your horse happen to win the race?" the visitor asked the jockey.

"Well, I just kept whispering in his ear," replied the jockey, "roses are red, violets are blue—horses that lose are made into glue."

The world is filled with failures—people who left good things only half-done.   —*O. A. Battista*

Electric shocks aren't entirely useless when the power goes off. They tell you exactly what happened.

If you don't invest very much, then defeat doesn't hurt very much and winning is not very exciting.
          —*Dick Vermeil*

People have different ways of responding to challenges. Some spit on their hands, grit their teeth, and throw themselves headlong into them. Some butt their heads against a brick wall. Some laugh helplessly and shrug their shoulders. Some blow their tops. Some declare the challenge is not worth bothering about. Still others sit back and drink the cup of bitterness, predicting failure—and virtually ensuring it.
          —*Sherwood Wirt*

It's not the big failures one minds so much; it's the constant pitter-patter of little defeats.

A winner never quits and a quitter never wins.

When an archer misses the mark, he turns and looks for the fault within himself. Failure to hit the bull's-eye is never the fault of the target. To improve your aim—improve yourself.   —*Gilbert Arland*

There is the greatest practical benefit in making a few failures early in life.

Failure is the path of least persistence.

The train of failure usually runs on the track of laziness.

If you can walk, you can run. No one is ever hurt. Hurt is in your mind.   —*Vince Lombardi*

In war there is no substitute for victory.
                                   —*Douglas MacArthur*

Wars may be fought with weapons, but they are won by men. It is the spirit of the men who follow and of the man who leads that gains the victory.
                                   —*George Patton, Jr.*

If you can accept losing, you can't win.

Winning is not a sometime thing; it's an all-time thing.

You don't win once in a while, you don't do things once in a while, you do them right all the time.

Winning is a habit.

Unfortunately, so is losing.   *—Vince Lombardi*

If you want a sure prescription for defeat it is this: play it safe, stifle your thoughts, hold your tongue and flatten your intellectual profile.
   —Thomas J. Watson, Jr.

A man can fail many times but he isn't a failure until he begins to blame somebody else.

Losers bemoan and bewail their blunders; winners bounce back in spite of their bloopers and boners.
   —William A. Ward

Ninety-nine percent of the failures come from people who have the habit of making excuses.

Failures are divided into two classes—those who thought and never did, and those who did and never thought.   *—John Charles Salak*

A great pleasure in life is doing what people say you
cannot do.   —*Walter Gagehot*

The road to failure is greased with the slime of
indifference.

Winners expect to win in advance. Life is a self-
fulfilling prophecy.

Don't Be Afraid to Fail ...
You've failed many times, although you may not
        remember.
You fell down the first time you tried to walk.
You almost drowned the first time you tried to
        swim, didn't you?
Did you hit the ball the first time you swung a bat?
Heavy hitters, the ones who hit the most home runs,
        also strike out a lot.
R. H. Macy failed seven times before his store in
        New York caught on.
English novelist John Creasey got 753 rejection slips
        before he published 564 books.
Babe Ruth struck out 1,330 times, but he also hit 714
        home runs.
Don't worry about failure. Worry about the chances
        you miss when you don't even try.
                                        —*Author unknown*

In great attempts it is glorious even to fail.

The man who wins may have been counted out several times, but he didn't hear the referee.

—*H. E. Jansen*

Winner Versus Loser
The winner—is always part of the answer;
The loser—is always part of the problem;
The winner—always has a program·
The loser—always has an excuse;
The winner—says, "Let me do it for you";
The loser—says, "That's not my job";
The winner—sees an answer for every problem;
The loser—sees a problem for every answer;
The winner—sees a green near every sand trap;
The loser—sees two or three sand traps near every
    green;
The winner—says, "It may be difficult but it's
    possible";
The loser—says, "It may be possible but it's too
    difficult."
Be a winner!

The men who try to do something and fail are infinitely better than those who try to do nothing and succeed.   —*Lloyd Jones*

Failure is the opportunity to begin again more
intelligently.   —*Henry Ford*

Success is simply a matter of luck; ask any failure.

You never fail until you stop trying.

Faith

The strengthening of faith comes through staying
with it in the hour of trial.   —*Catherine Marshall*

Faith is telling a mountain to move and being
shocked only if it doesn't.

Faith, in its very nature, demands action. Faith is
action—never a passive attitude.   —*Paul E. Little*

If doubt overtakes you, stop for a faith lift.

Fear knocked at the door. Faith answered. No one
was there.

Faith comes by hearing, and hearing by the word of
God.   —*The Apostle Paul (Romans 10:17, NKJ)*

Doubt sees the obstacles, faith sees the way;
doubt sees the darkest night, faith sees the day;
doubt dreads to take a step, faith soars on high;
doubt questions, "Who believes?" while faith
answers "*I.*"

Pin your faith on no man's sleeve; have faith in God.

Faith hears the inaudible, sees the invisible, believes
the incredible, and receives the impossible.

All I have seen teaches me to trust the Creator for all
I have not seen.   —*Ralph Waldo Emerson*

Faith is not a pill you take but a muscle you use.

Faith draws the poison from every grief, takes the
sting from every loss and quenches the fire of every
pain.

Faith and conviction become stronger when attacked.

Faith says, "I will give it before I get it."

Real faith is not the stuff dreams are made of; rather
it is tough, practical and altogether realistic. Faith
sees the invisible but it does not see the nonexistent.
                                           —*A. W. Tozer*

He who prays for rain should always carry an umbrella.

It is impossible for faith to overdraw its account on the bank of heaven.

Feed your faith and your doubts will starve to death.

Let us have faith that right makes might, and in that faith let us, to the end, dare to do our duty as we understand it.   —*Abraham Lincoln*

Faith is to the watching soul what a mainspring is to a watch.

Three men were walking on a wall—
Feeling, Faith and Fact.
Feeling took an awful fall,
And Faith was taken back.
Faith was so close to Feeling
That he then fell down too,
But Fact remained and pulled Faith up,
And Faith brought Feeling too.

Both faith and fear sail into the harbor of your mind, but only faith should be allowed to anchor.

For if you have faith even as small as a tiny mustard seed you could say to this mountain, "Move!" and it would go far away. Nothing would be impossible.
—Jesus (Matthew 17:20)

Faith can rewrite your future.

You can never please God without faith, without depending on him. Anyone who wants to come to God must believe there is a God and that he rewards those who sincerely look for him.
—The Apostle Paul (Hebrews 11:6)

Pray for faith that will not shrink when it is washed in the waters of affliction.   *—Ernest Wadsworth*

Sorrow looks back. Worry looks around. Faith looks up.

Faith is the daring of the soul to go farther than it can see.

Faith, mighty faith, the promise sees
and looks to God alone,
laughs at impossibilities,
and cries, "It shall be done."   *—Charles Wesley*

Family

If anyone does not provide for his relatives, and especially for his own family, he has disowned the faith and is worse than an unbeliever.
>   —*The Apostle Paul (1 Timothy 5:8, RSV)*

Where does the family start? It starts with a young man in love with a girl—no superior alternative has yet been found.   —*Winston Churchill*

He gives families to the lonely, and releases prisoners from jail.   —*Psalms 68:6*

The fool who provokes his family to anger and resentment will finally have nothing worthwhile left. He shall be the servant of a wiser man.
>   —*Solomon (Proverbs 11:29)*

All that I am, or hope to be, I owe to my angel mother.   —*Abraham Lincoln*

My mother was the most beautiful woman I ever saw. All I am I owe to my mother.
>   —*George Washington*

All that I am my mother made me.
> —*John Quincy Adams*

Since a child at my mother's knee, I have believed in honor, ethics and right living for its own reward.
> —*Harry S. Truman*

My best training came from my father.
> —*Woodrow Wilson*

My father's interest in politics made him the most enthusiastic follower of my career from its beginnings.
> —*Richard Nixon*

My father was the dominant person in our family and in my life.
> —*Jimmy Carter*

A good name and good advice is all your dad can give you.
> —*Harry S. Truman*

As a substitute father for hundreds of youths over the past thirteen years, I have yet to encounter a young person in trouble whose difficulty could not be traced to the lack of a strong father-image in the home.
> —*Paul Anderson*

The father is the head of the house; the mother is the heart of the house.

While I don't minimize the vital role played by a mother, I believe a successful family begins with her husband.   —*James Dobson*

Could I turn back the time machine, I would double the attention I gave my children and go to fewer meetings.   —*J. D. Eppinga*

What a father says to his children is not heard by the world, but it will be heard by posterity.
                                  —*Jean Paul Richter*

There are a great many fathers who tie up their hound dog at night and let their boys run loose.

If mothers would understand that much of their importance lies in building up the father image for the child, the children would turn out well.
                                  —*Samuel S. Liebowitz*

The chances are that you will never be elected president of the country, write the great American novel, make a million dollars, stop pollution and racial conflict, or save the world. However valid it may be to work at any of these goals, there is another one of higher priority—to be an effective parent.
                                  —*Landrum R. Bolling*

Let every Christian father and mother understand
when the child is three years old that they have done
more than half they will ever do for his character.

The experts and I
Can never agree.
They say children are ruined
Before they are three.
But I'll keep on trying
I'll valiantly strive
To rehabilitate Junior
Before he is five.
                                        —*Louise Darcy*

It is easier to build boys than to mend men.

If discipline were practiced in every home, juvenile
delinquency would be reduced by 95 percent.
                                        —*J. Edgar Hoover*

(Good parents are) not afraid to be momentarily
disliked by children during the act of enforcing rules.
                                        —*Jean Laird*

The actions of some children today suggest that their
parents embarked upon the sea of matrimony
without a paddle.

A child's back must be made to bend, but not be broken. He must be ruled, but not with a rod of iron. His spirit must be conquered, but not crushed.
                                                —*Charles Spurgeon*

Children are the sum of what parents contribute to their lives.   —*Richard L. Strauss*

Parents spend half their time wondering how their children will turn out, and half the time wondering when they will turn in.

Little children, headache; big children, heartache.
                                                —*Italian proverb*

Childhood—that wonderful time when all you need to do to lose weight is to bathe.

Youth—those who are always ready to give to those older than themselves the full benefit of their experience.   —*Oscar Wilde*

The rules for parents
are but three . . .
Love,
Limit,
And let them be!   —*Elaine M. Ward*

Children—our most valuable resource.
—*Herbert Hoover*

The trouble with parenthood is that by the time you're experienced, you're unemployable.

Children aren't happy with nothing to ignore, and that's what parents are created for.   —*Ogden Nash*

Blueprint

Home—a world of strife shut out, a world of love shut in.

Home—a place where the small are great, and the great are small.

Home—the father's kingdom, the mother's world, and the child's paradise.

Home—the place where we grumble the most, and are treated the best.

Home—the center of our affection, round which our heart's best wishes twine.

Home—the place where our stomachs get three square meals a day and our hearts a thousand.
—*Charles M. Crowe*

Home is where you go when other places close.
—*Joseph Laurie*

Home—the place where, when you go there, they
have to take you in.   —*Robert Frost*

Home—a place we go to change our clothes so as to
go somewhere else.   —*Elbert Hubbard*

House—the thing that keeps a man running to the
hardware store.   —*Robert Zwickery*

A Father's Prayer
Build me a son, O Lord, who will be strong enough
to know when he is weak, and brave enough to face
himself when he is afraid; one who will be proud
and unbending in honest defeat, and humble and
gentle in victory.

Build me a son whose wishbone will not be where
his backbone should be; a son who will know thee
and that to know himself is the foundation stone of
knowledge.

Lead him, I pray, not in the path of ease and comfort,
but under stress and spur of difficulties and challenge. Here let him learn to stand up in the storm;
here let him learn compassion for those who fail.

Build me a son whose heart will be clear, whose goal
will be high; a son who will master himself before he
seeks to master other men; one who will learn to

laugh, yet never forget how to weep; one who will reach into the future, yet never forget the past.

And after all these things are his, add, I pray, enough of a sense of humor, so that he may always be serious, yet never take himself too seriously. Give him humility, so that he may always remember the simplicity of true greatness, the open mind of true wisdom, the meekness of true strength.

Then I, his father, will dare to whisper, "I have not lived in vain."
                                        —*Douglas MacArthur*

Forgiveness

Never build your preaching of forgiveness on the fact that God is our Father and He will forgive us because He loves us . . . It is shallow nonsense to say that God forgives us because He is love. The only ground on which God can forgive me is through the cross of my Lord.
                                        —*Oswald Chambers*

Be kind to one another, tenderhearted, forgiving one another, as God in Christ forgave you.
            —*The Apostle Paul (Ephesians 4:32, RSV)*

He who cannot forgive breaks the bridge over which he himself must pass.   —*George Herbert*

"I can forgive, but I cannot forget," is only another way of saying, "I will not forgive."

If His conditions are met, God is bound by His Word to forgive any man or any woman of any sin because of Christ.   —*Billy Graham*

Forgiving those who hurt us is the key to personal peace.   —*G. Weatherly*

Forgiveness is simply giving up your right to exact the penalty for the wrong done you, refusing to take revenge. In the Christian's view, it is allowing Jesus' crucifixion to pay not only for your sin, but the sin of another against you.
                    —*Jim A. Talley and Jane Carlile Baker*

A Christian will find it cheaper to pardon than to resent. Forgiveness saves the expense of anger, the cost of hatred, the waste of spirits.   —*Hannah More*

Never does the human soul appear so strong and noble as when it foregoes revenge and dares to forgive an injury.   —*E. H. Chapin*

Forgiveness is the answer to the child's dream of a miracle by which what is broken is made whole again, what is soiled is again made clean.

—Dag Hammarskjöld

Of him that hopes to be forgiven it is required that he forgive ... On this great duty eternity is suspended; and to him that refuses to practice it the throne of mercy is inaccessible, and the Saviour of the world has been born in vain. *—Johnson*

Friends

To a Friend
I love you, not only for what you are,
    but for what I am
    when I am with you.
I love you, not only for what
    you have made of yourself,
    but for what
    you are making of me.
I love you
    for the part of me
    that you bring out;

I love you
    for putting your hand
    into my heaped-up heart
    and passing over
    all the foolish, weak things
    that you can't help
    dimly seeing there,
    and for drawing
    out into the light
    all the beautiful belongings
    that no one else had looked
    quite far enough to find.
I love you for ignoring the possibilities of the fool
    and weakling in me, and for laying firm hold on
    the possibilities of the good in me.
I love you for closing your ears to the discords in me,
    and for adding to the music in me by worshipful
    listening.
I love you because you
    are helping me to make
    of the lumber of my life
    not a tavern,
    but a temple;
    out of the works
    of my every day
    not a reproach
    but a song.

I love you
  because you have done
  more than any creed
  could have done
  to make me good,
  and more than any fate
  could have done
  to make me happy.
You have done it without a touch,
  without a word,
  without a sign.
  You have done it
  by being yourself.
  Perhaps that is what
  being a friend means,
  after all.   *—Roy Croft*

Am I not destroying my enemies when I make
friends of them?   *—Abraham Lincoln*

A real friend is one who will tell you of your faults
and follies in prosperity, and assist with his hand and
heart in adversity.

There are three things that grow more precious with
age: old wood to burn, old books to read, and old
friends to enjoy.

My best friend is the one who brings out the best in
me.   —*Henry Ford*

Friends are God's life preservers.

You cannot shake hands with a clenched fist.
                                               —*Golda Meir*

What Is a Friend?
An English publication offered a prize for the best
definition of a friend, and among the thousands of
answers received were the following:

"One who multiplies joys, divides grief, and whose
    honesty is inviolable."
"One who understands our silence."
"A volume of sympathy bound in cloth."
"A watch which beats true for all time and never runs
    down."
Here is the definition that won the prize: "A friend is
the one who comes in when the whole world has
gone out."

A true friend is always loyal, and a brother is born to
help in time of need.   —*Solomon (Proverbs 17:17)*

The trouble with being a grouch is that you have to
make new friends every few months.

If I Had Known

If I had known what trouble you were bearing,
What griefs were in the silence of your face;
I would have been more gentle, and more caring,
And tried to give you gladness for a space.
I would have brought more warmth into the place,
If I had known.

If I had known what thoughts despairing drew you;
(Why do we never try to understand?)
I would have lent a little friendship to you,
And slipped my hand within your hand,
And made your stay more pleasant in the land,
If I had known.   —*Mary Carolyn Davies*

Speak well of your enemies—you made them.

There is a saying, "Love your friends and hate your
enemies." But I say: Love your enemies! Pray for
those who persecute you! In that way you will be
acting as true sons of your Father in heaven. For he
gives his sunlight to both the evil and the good, and
sends rain on the just and on the unjust too.
                        —*Jesus (Matthew 5:43–45)*

Real friends are those who, when you've made a fool
of yourself, don't feel that you've done a permanent
job.

An evil man sows strife; gossip separates the best of
friends.   —*Solomon (Proverbs 16:28)*

The best way to wipe out a friendship is to sponge
on it.

Be slow in choosing a friend, slower in changing.
                                        —*Benjamin Franklin*

Faithful are the wounds of a friend; but the kisses of
an enemy are deceitful. —*Solomon (Proverbs 27:6, KJV)*

Before borrowing money from a friend decide which
you need most.   —*American proverb*

Three things we can all do today;
To pause a moment just to pray,
To be a friend both tried and true
And find some good that we can do.
                                        —*William A. Ward*

A friend is someone who understands your past,
believes in your future, and accepts you today just
the way you are.

A friendly discussion is as stimulating as the sparks
that fly when iron strikes iron.
                                        —*Solomon (Proverbs 27:17)*

He who walks in when others walk out is a true friend.

The best way to test a man's friendship is to ask him to go on your note. If he refuses, he is your friend.

Be slow to fall into friendship, but when thou art in, continue firm and constant.   —*Socrates*

The best way to keep your friends is not to give them away.

There are good ships, and there are bad ships, but the best ships are friendships.

Friendship adds a brighter radiance to prosperity and lightens the burden of adversity by dividing and sharing it.   —*Cicero*

Grief can take care of itself, but to get the full value of joy, you must have a friend with whom to share it.

If you want an accounting of your worth, count your friends.   —*Merry Browne*

It is one of the most beautiful compensations of this life that no man can sincerely try to help another without helping himself.   —*Ralph W. Emerson*

Real friends don't care if your socks don't match.

Those who bring sunshine to the lives of others cannot keep it from themselves.

Money can't buy friends, but it will buy a better class of enemies.

Your friend is your field which you sow with love and reap with thanksgiving.   *—Gibran*

Look around today and share a cheerful, friendly smile; show the world you truly care, then go the second mile.   *—William A. Ward*

There's a special kind of freedom friends enjoy. Freedom to share innermost thoughts, to ask a favor, to show their true feelings. The freedom to simply be themselves.

Fulfillment
(also Satisfaction)

Fulfillment doesn't automatically happen as a result of linking up with the "right" person, job, or even

ministry. Fulfillment happens as a result of being in
God's will.   —*Marilyn Olson*

Only God can fully satisfy the hungry heart of man.
                                               —*Hugh Black*

Thou wilt shew me the path of life: in thy presence is
fullness of joy; at thy right hand there are pleasures
for evermore.   —*Psalm 16:11 (KJV)*

Five keys to fulfilling living:
1. Obey a great God.
2. Dream great dreams.
3. Plan great plans.
4. Pray great prayers.
5. Claim great victories.

He is well paid that is well satisfied.
                                        —*William Shakespeare*

In the world there are only two tragedies. One is not
getting what one wants, and the other is getting it.
                                               —*Oscar Wilde*

Life's greatest satisfactions include getting the last
laugh, having the last word, and paying the last
installment.

If you don't get everything you want, think of the things you don't get that you don't want.

Make a rule, and pray to God to help you to keep it, never, if possible, to lie down at night without being able to say: "I have made one human being a little wiser, or a little happier, or at least a little better this day."   —*Charles Kingsley*

He who chooses a job he likes will never have to work a day in his life.

Almost anything can be bought at a reduced price except lasting satisfaction.

Few things in life are more satisfying than parking on what's left of the other person's quarter.

Telling the truth gives a man great satisfaction, and hard work returns many blessings to him.
                                        —*Solomon (Proverbs 12:14)*

Fulfillment is not a true goal to pursue. It is a by-product of our completeness.   —*Malcolm Nygren*

The reward of a thing well done is to have done it.
                                        —*Ralph W. Emerson*

Unless each day can be looked back upon by an individual as one in which he has had some fun, some joy, some real satisfaction, that day is a loss. It is un-Christian and wicked, in my opinion, to allow such a thing to occur.　　　　　*—Dwight D. Eisenhower*

There is no satisfaction in hanging a man who does not object to it.　　　　　*—George Bernard Shaw*

A wise friend once told me that when you have certain gifts you might be denied other things. The only thing no one can allow himself to be denied is a sense of satisfaction. Everyone needs to achieve regularly a sense of satisfaction, perhaps as a counterbalance to our sense of responsibility.　　*—Danny Kaye*

The Future
(see also Dreams)

He who provides for this life, but takes no care for eternity, is wise for a moment, but a fool forever.
　　　　　　　—John Tillotson

The future is history with God, for He is omniscient.

Tomorrow is the day that's always on its way, yet never arrives—unless you have a payment due then.

The worst thing about the future is that it seems to get here quicker than it used to.

Perhaps the best thing about the future is that it comes just one day at a time.

Notice on college bulletin board: "Owing to unforseen circumstances our course—*Predicting Your Future*—has had to be canceled."

One thing the future *can* guarantee—anything can happen.

The future belongs to those who prepare for it.

Never put off until tomorrow what you can do today. If you wait until tomorrow, they will probably have passed a law prohibiting it.

The wise man saves for the future, but the foolish man spends whatever he gets.
> —*Solomon (Proverbs 21:20)*

There is nothing like a dream to create the future.
> —*Victor Hugo*

About the only thing that comes to him who waits is old age. No one can build a reputation on what he's going to do tomorrow.

My interest is in the future because I'm going to spend the rest of my life there.

The trouble with our times is that the future is not what it used to be. —*Paul Valery*

If we open a quarrel between the past and the present, we shall find we have lost the future.
—*Winston Churchill*

I like the dreams of the future better than the history of the past. —*Thomas Jefferson*

January 1: "I resolve to be optimistic about the future—if there is one."

Hats off to the past; sleeves up for the future.

The future always holds something for the man who keeps his faith in it. —*H. L. Hollis*

Enjoy present pleasures in such a way as not to injure future ones.

Where you go hereafter depends on what you go
after here.

He gave her a smile with a future in it.

I Have Found Today
I've shut the door on Yesterday,
Its sorrows and mistakes;
I've locked within its gloomy walls
Past failures and heartaches,
And now I throw the key away
To seek another room,
And furnish it with hope and smiles
And every springtime bloom.

No thought shall enter this abode
That has a hint of pain,
And worry, malice and distrust
Shall never therein reign.
I've shut the door on Yesterday
and thrown the key away—
Tomorrow holds no doubt for me,
Since I have found today.

Never be afraid to trust an unknown future to an
all-knowing God.   —*Corrie ten Boom*

Goals
(also Ideals, Purpose)

My Purpose
To awaken each morning with a smile brightening
my face;
To greet the day with reverence for the opportunities
it contains;
To approach my work with a clean mind;
To hold ever before me, even in the doing of little
things, the Ultimate Purpose toward which I am
working;
To meet men and women with laughter on my lips
and love in my heart;
To be gentle and kind, and courteous through all the
hours;
To approach the night with weariness that ever
woos sleep, and the joy that comes from work
well done—
This is how I desire to waste wisely my days.
—*Thomas Dekker*

A teenager complained to a friend: "My dad wants
me to have all the things he never had when he was
a boy—including five straight *A*'s on my report card."

Long-range goals keep you from being frustrated by
short-term failures.

Aim for a goal and start on your way,
it may take a year, or only a day.
Travel slowly and watch for mistakes—
don't worry about the time it takes.
The path may be rough and mostly uphill;
but you'll get to the top by using your will.

Goals—write them down; hang them up; and with
God's help, watch them happen!

Choose a goal for which you are willing to exchange
a piece of your life.

The poor man is not he who is without a cent, but he
who is without a dream.   —*Harry Kemp*

It's more important to know where you're going,
than to see how fast you can get there.

Our plans miscarry because they have no aim. When
a man does not know what harbor he is making for,
no wind is the right wind.

There's no point aiming at a target with no arrow in
your bow.

He who aims at nothing is sure to hit it.

Aim for the top. There is plenty of room here. There are so few at the top, it is almost lonely.
—Samuel Insull

Aim high but stay on the level.

Wisdom is the main pursuit of sensible men, but a fool's goals are at the ends of the earth.
—Solomon (Proverbs 17:24)

Climb high, climb far;
your aim the sky, your goal the star.

In the long run you hit only what you aim at. Therefore, though you should fail immediately, you had better aim at something high.   *—Henry Thoreau*

Life is a leaf of paper white
Whereon each one of us may write
His word or two,
And then comes night.

Greatly begin, though thou has time
But for a line,
Be that sublime,
Not failure, but low aim, is crime.

The majority see the obstacles; the few see the objectives; history records the successes of the latter, while oblivion is the reward of the former.

Have two goals: wisdom—that is, knowing and doing right—and common sense. Don't let them slip away, for they fill you with living energy, and are a feather in your cap.   —*Solomon (Proverbs 3:21,22)*

Too many people shoot blanks when aiming at their goals.

A man who is going nowhere can be sure of reaching his destination.

So I run straight to the goal with purpose in every step. I fight to win. I'm not just shadow-boxing or playing around.
                    —*The Apostle Paul (1 Corinthians 9:26)*

There's no point carrying the ball if you don't know where the goal is.

Five worthy goals: a healthy body, a clear conscience, a courageous heart, an inquiring mind, and a questing spirit.   —*William A. Ward*

Obstacles are those frightful things you see when
you take your eyes off the goal.   —*Hannah More*

Ideals may be beyond our reach but never beyond
our fondest hopes.

Live your life each day as you would climb a
mountain.

An occasional glance toward the summit keeps the
goal in mind, but many beautiful scenes are to be
observed from each new vantage point.

Climb slowly, steadily, enjoying each passing
moment; and the view from the summit will serve
as a fitting climax for the journey.

—*Harold V. Melchert*

If you are satisfied with yourself, you had better
change your ideals.

Most of us serve our ideals by fits and starts. The
person who makes a success of living is the one who
sees his goal steadily and aims for it unswervingly.

—*Cecil B. de Mille*

Ideals are like tuning forks; you must sound them
frequently to keep your life up to pitch.

Our ideals are too often like an antique chair—nice to talk about and show off, but too fragile to use.

Clear definition of goals is the keynote of success.
                                              —*Edison Montgomery*

It's a sad fact that many politicians are more concerned with deals than with ideals.

Keep your ideals high enough to inspire you, and low enough to encourage you.

Happiness

I believe if a man sets an attainable goal for himself and works to attain it, conscious that when he does so he will then set another goal for himself, he will have a full, busy, and—for this reason—a happy life.
                                              —*Lionel Barrymore*

The grand essentials for happiness are: something to do, something to love, something to hope for.
                                              —*John Chalmers*

Most people are about as happy as they make up
their minds to be.   —*Abraham Lincoln*

The roots of happiness grow deepest in the soil of
service.

The secret of happy living is not to do what you like
but like what you do.

Happiness is the delicate balance between what one
is and what one has.   —*F. H. Denison*

Happiness is something that comes into our lives
through a door we don't remember leaving open.

It isn't our position but our disposition that makes us
happy.

He that is of a merry heart hath a continual feast.
          —*Solomon (Proverbs 15:15, KJV)*

Grudges are clots in the arteries leading to a happy
heart.   —*Frank Tyger*

If you ever find happiness by hunting for it, you will
find it, as the old woman did her lost spectacles, safe
on her own nose all the time.   —*Josh Billings*

Oh, the joys of those who do not follow evil men's
advice, who do not hang around with sinners, scoff-
ing at the things of God: But they delight in doing
everything God wants them to, and day and night
are always meditating on his laws and thinking about
ways to follow him more closely.

They are like trees along a river bank, bearing lus-
cious fruit each season without fail. Their leaves shall
never wither, and all they do shall prosper.

—Psalm 1:1–3

Happiness is a rebound from hard work.

Happiness is not a station to arrive at, but a manner
of traveling.   *—Margaret Lee Runbeck*

The really happy man is the one who can enjoy the
scenery even when he has to take a detour.

Happiness is not the absence of conflict, but the
ability to cope with it.

Happiness is a direction not a destination.

Indeed, a man wishes to be happy even when he so
lives as to make happiness impossible.

—St. Augustine

A merry heart doeth good like a medicine.
—*Solomon (Proverbs 17:22, KJV)*

Happy is the housewife who sees the rainbows, not the dishes, in the soapsuds.

Happiness is a way station between too much and too little.

Happiness is the inner joy that can be sought or caught, but never taught or bought.

Many indeed think of being happy with God in heaven, but being happy with God on earth never enters their minds. —*John Wesley*

In the pursuit of happiness, the difficulty lies in knowing when you have caught up. —*R. H. Grenville*

The U.S. Constitution doesn't guarantee happiness, only the pursuit of it. You have to catch up to it yourself. —*Benjamin Franklin*

Bride's father to the groom: "My boy, you're the second happiest man in the world."

Happiness is discovering that the slip of paper under your windshield is just an advertisement.

The road to happiness is always under construction.

The thing that counts most in pursuit of happiness is choosing the right traveling companion.

Happiness is hiring a babysitter who is on a diet.

Happiness is having a scratch for every itch.
                                              —*Ogden Nash*

One man's admission: "I'm happy to live in a free country where a man can do what his wife pleases."

A small house will hold as much happiness as a big one.

Pleasant sights and good reports give happiness and health.   —*Solomon (Proverbs 15:30)*

The surest way to happiness is in losing yourself in a cause greater than yourself.

For every minute you are angry, you lose sixty seconds of happiness.

A man has happiness in the palm of his hands if he can fill his days with real work and his nights with real rest.

Genuine happiness occurs when a wife sees a double chin on her husband's old girlfriend.

The heart is happiest when it beats for others.

Happy is the man with a level-headed son; sad the mother of a rebel. —*Solomon (Proverbs 10:1)*

Happiness is like a potato salad—when shared with others, it's a picnic.

Nothing gives a man greater pleasure than doing a good deed in secret and having it found out by accident.

Happiness is making a bouquet of those flowers within reach.

The secret of happiness is not in doing what one likes, but in liking what one has to do.

The only ones among you who will be truly happy are those who will have sought and found how to serve. —*Albert Schweitzer*

Wisdom is a tree of life to those who eat her fruit; happy is the man who keeps on eating it.
—*Solomon (Proverbs 3:18)*

Happiness is a by-product of an effort to make someone else happy.   —*Gretta Palmer*

Honesty

I hope that I shall always possess firmness and virtue
enough to maintain what I consider the most envi-
able of all titles: the character of an honest man.
                    —*George Washington*

Make yourself an honest man and then you may be
sure there is one rascal less in the world.
                    —*Thomas Carlyle*

I do not know what the heart of a rascal may be, but
I do know what is in the heart of an honest man; it is
horrible.   —*Joseph de Maistre*

To be honest, as this world goes, is to be one man
picked out of ten thousand.   —*William Shakespeare*

Any story sounds true until someone tells the other
side and sets the record straight.
                    —*Solomon (Proverbs 18:17)*

There are no such people as honest people, there are
only people less crooked.   —*Gerald F. Lieberman.*

A little, gained honestly, is better than great wealth
gotten by dishonest means. —*Solomon (Proverbs 16:8)*

An honest executive is one who shares the credit
with the man who did all the work.

He that resolves to deal with none but honest men
must leave off dealing.   —*Thomas Fuller*

It is a wonderful heritage to have an honest father.
                                —*Solomon (Proverbs 20:7)*

Honesty is largely a matter of information, of knowing that dishonesty is a mistake. Principle is not as
powerful in keeping people straight as a policeman.
                                —*Edgar Watson Howe*

An honest man is the noblest work of God.
                                —*Alexander Pope*

It takes an honest man to tell whether he's tired or
just lazy.

Dishonest gain will never last, so why take the risk?
                                —*Solomon (Proverbs 21:6)*

Draw your salary before spending it.   *—George Ade*

If you tell the truth, you don't have to remember
anything.   *—Mark Twain*

Better to be poor and honest than rich and dishonest.
                                —Solomon (Proverbs 19:1)

Campaigning for public office, my husband pre-
sented one of his cards to an Italian woman in
Monterey, California. His picture was on it, along
with information about his background and the
office he was seeking.

The lady looked at the card, then at my husband.
"Yes," she said decisively, "I vote for you—a bald-
headed man who has his picture taken without his
hat is an honest man."

Lock your door and keep your neighbor honest.
                                    —Chinese proverb

Never forget to be truthful and kind. Hold these
virtues tightly.   *—Solomon (Proverbs 3:3)*

I don't want a bunch of yes-men around me. I want
people to tell me the truth—even if it costs them
their job.   *—Samuel Goldwyn*

Regardless of policy, honesty is easier on the nerves.

Honesty is the first chapter in the book of wisdom.
                                        —*Thomas Jefferson*

So live your life that your autograph will be wanted instead of your fingerprints.

The world will be a better place to live in when the "found" ads in the newspapers begin to outnumber the "lost" ads.

Lies will get any man into trouble, but honesty is its own defense.   —*Solomon (Proverbs 12:13)*

Honor

He has honor if he holds himself to an ideal of conduct though it is inconvenient, unprofitable, or dangerous to do so.   —*Walter Lippmann*

If I honor myself, my honor is nothing.
                                        —*John (8:54, KJV)*

Honor lies in honest toil.   —*Grover Cleveland*

The louder he talked of his honor, the faster we
counted our spoons.   —*Ralph Waldo Emerson*

Professor: "Now, this examination will be conducted
on the honor system. Please take seats three seats
apart, in alternate rows, and we shall begin."

Honor your father and your mother.
                                   —*Exodus 20:12 (RSV)*

I feel it is time that I also pay tribute to my four
writers—Matthew, Mark, Luke and John.
                                   —*Bishop Fulton J. Sheen*

It is an honor to receive a frank reply.
                                   —*Solomon (Proverbs 24:26)*

Even honor and virtue make enemies, condemning,
as they do, their opposites by too close a contrast.
                                   —*Tacutys*

It is a badge of honor to accept valid criticism.
                                   —*Solomon (Proverbs 25:12)*

That nation is worthless that will not, with pleasure,
venture all for its honor.   —*Schiller*

Humility and reverence for the Lord will make you both wise and honored.   —*Solomon (Proverbs 15:33)*

Hope

Of all the forces that make for a better world, none is so indispensable, none so powerful, as hope. Without hope men are only half alive.   —*Charles Sawyer*

Faith plus hope is powerful.

The best bridge between hope and despair is often a good night's sleep.

Never live in hope or expectation with your arms folded.

He who has health has hope, and he who has hope has everything.

Probably nothing in the world arouses more false hopes than the first four hours of a diet.
                                                     —*Dan Bennett*

Where hope is gone, defeat prevails.

Hope deferred makes the heart sick; but when
dreams come true at last, there is life and joy.
                              —*Solomon (Proverbs 13:12)*

Hope smiles on the threshold of the year to some,
whispering that it will be happier.
                              —*Alfred, Lord Tennyson*

Blessed is the man who trusts in the Lord and has
made the Lord his hope and confidence.
                              —*Jeremiah (17:7)*

As we journey through life the thing we long for is
hope. There is no greater source of hope than God's
Word.   —*Sandi Patti*

Hope, like the gleaming taper's light,
Adorns and cheers our way;
And still, as darker grows the night,
Emits a lighter ray.   —*Oliver Goldsmith*

We are never beneath hope, while above hell; nor
above hope, while beneath heaven.

Hope springs eternal in the human breast;
Man never is, but always to be blest.
                              —*Alexander Pope*

He who lives in hope dances without a fiddle.

Hope is grief's best music.

No affliction nor temptation, no guilt nor power of
sin, no wounded spirit nor terrified conscience,
should induce us to despair of help and comfort from
God.   —*T. Scott*

And now abideth faith, hope, charity, these three;
but the greatest of these is charity.
                    —*The Apostle Paul (1 Corinthians 13:13, KJV)*

It is certainly wrong to despair; and if despair is
wrong, hope is right.   —*John Lubbock*

Sam: Have you ever realized any of your childhood
hopes?

Cam: Yes, when mother used to comb my hair, I
often wished I didn't have any.

When you say a situation or a person is hopeless,
you are slamming the door in the face of God.
                                               —*Charles L. Allen*

The heart bowed down by weight of woe to
weakest hope will cling.   —*Alfred Bunn*

Lost hope is the undertaker's best friend.

Hope is the feeling that you will succeed tomorrow in what you failed at today.

While there is life there is hope.   —*Latin proverb*

He brought light out of darkness, not out of a lesser light; He can bring your summer out of winter, though you have no spring; though in the ways of fortune, or understanding, or conscience, you have been benighted until now, wintered and frozen, clouded and eclipsed, damped and benumbed, smothered and stupefied till now, now God comes to you, not as in the dawning of the day, not as in the bid of the spring, but as the sun at noon.
                                      —*John Donne*

Humility

Pride ends in destruction; humility ends in honor.
                    —*Solomon (Proverbs 18:12)*

Few things are as humbling as a three-way mirror.

Humility is perfect quietness of heart. It is to expect nothing, to wonder at nothing that is done to me, to feel nothing done against me. It is to be at rest when nobody praises me, and when I am blamed or despised. —*Andrew Murray*

As the nightingale instinctively flees from the sound of the hawk, so does the beauty of humility vanish in the presence of pride. —*William A. Ward*

Pride leads to arguments; be humble, take advice and become wise. —*Solomon (Proverbs 13:10)*

Humility is a strange thing; the moment you think you have it you have lost it.

Humility is to make the right estimate of yourself. —*Charles Spurgeon*

Your attitude should be the kind that was shown us by Jesus Christ, who, though he was God, did not demand and cling to his rights as God, but laid aside his mighty power and glory. And he humbled himself. —*The Apostle Paul (Philippians 2:5–8)*

Don't be humble; you're not that great. —*Golda Meir*

I used to think that God's gifts were on shelves—one above another—and the taller we grow, the easier we can reach them. Now I find that God's gifts are on shelves—one beneath the other—and the lower we stoop, the more we get.   —*F. B. Meyer*

The fellow who does things that count doesn't usually stop to count them.

One of the hardest secrets for a man to keep is his opinion of himself.

And whosoever shall exalt himself shall be abased; and he that shall humble himself shall be exalted.
                              —*Matthew (23:12, KJV)*

To be humble to superiors is duty; to equals, courtesy; to inferiors, nobility.

Those traveling the highway of humility won't be bothered by any heavy traffic.

Sincere humility attracts. Lack of humility subtracts. Artificial humility detracts.

Humility is like underwear—essential, but indecent if it shows.   —*Helen Nielson*

God created the world out of nothing, and as long as we are nothing, He can make something out of us.
—*Martin Luther*

True humility and respect for the Lord lead a man to riches, honor and long life.   —*Solomon (Proverbs 22:4)*

If anyone would like to acquire humility, I can, I think, tell him the first step. The first step is to realize that one is proud. And a biggish step too.
—*C. S. Lewis*

If you will humble yourselves under the mighty hand of God, in his good time he will lift you up.
—*Peter (1 Peter 5:6)*

Humility is remaining teachable.

Humble tasks
I long to accomplish a great and noble task, but it is my chief duty to accomplish humble tasks as though they were great and noble. The world is moved along, not only by the mighty shoves of its heroes, but also by the aggregate of the tiny pushes of each honest worker.   —*Helen Keller*

Humor

Give me a sense of humor, Lord;
Give me the grace to see a joke,
To get some happiness from life
And pass it on to other folk.

Laughter is the sun that drives winter from the
human face.   —*Victor Hugo*

The best sense of humor belongs to the fellow who
can laugh at himself.

With the fearful strain that is on me night and day, if
I did not laugh I should die.   —*Abraham Lincoln*

Humor is to life what shock absorbers are to
automobiles.

Humor is the hole that lets the sawdust out of a
stuffed shirt.

The Bible speaks of a time when all tears shall be
wiped away. But it makes no mention of a time
when we shall cease to smile.   —*J. D. Eppinga*

Get well cards have become so humorous that if you don't get sick you're missing a lot of fun.

I would have less wish to go to heaven if I knew that God would not understand a joke.   —*Martin Luther*

Laugh at yourself first, before anyone else can.
                                              —*Elsa Maxwell*

The humorist has a good eye for the humbug; he does not always recognize the saint.
                                        —*W. Somerset Maugham*

A sense of humor is the pole that adds balance to our steps as we walk the tightrope of life.
                                          —*William A. Ward*

A sense of humor reduces people and problems to their proper proportions.

Humor is the lubricating oil of business. It prevents friction and wins good will.

After God created the world, he made man and woman. Then, to keep the whole thing from collapsing, he invented humor.   —*Guillermo Mordillo*

Humor is the lifeboat we use on life's river.

Our five senses are incomplete without the sixth—a sense of humor.

On a school bulletin board: Laugh and the class laughs with you, but you stay after school alone.

Laughing is the sensation of feeling good all over and showing it principally in one spot.   —*Josh Billings*

If you can look in the mirror without laughing, you have no sense of humor.

When you think about having a woman for President, that's no problem. What's worrisome is the thought of having a man for First Lady.

I never lack material for my humor column when Congress is in session.   —*Will Rogers*

Laughter is part of the human survival kit.
                                         —*David Nathan*

The saving grace of America lies in the fact that the overwhelming majority of Americans are possessed of two great qualities—a sense of humor and a sense of proportion.   —*Franklin D. Roosevelt*

Laughter is a tranquilizer with no side effects.
—*Arnold Glasgow*

Kindness

I expect to pass through the world but once. Any good therefore that I can do, or any kindness that I can show to any fellow creature, let me do it now. Let me not defer it or neglect it, for I shall not pass this way again.   —*Stephen Grellet (attr.)*

Kindness consists of loving people more than they deserve.   —*Joseph Joubert*

Kindness makes a man attractive.
—*Solomon (Proverbs 19:22)*

The one who knows how to show and to accept kindness will be a friend better than any possession.
—*Sophocles*

There are three rules of dealing with all those who come to us: 1. Kindness; 2. Kindness; 3. Kindness.
—*Fulton J. Sheen*

The man who grows roses in his garden does a kindness to his neighbors.

True kindness presupposes the faculty of imagining as one's own the suffering and joys of others.
                                                —*André Gide*

Kindness can become its own motive. We are made kind by being kind.   —*Eric Hoffer*

If a king is kind, honest and fair, his kingdom stands secure.   —*Solomon (Proverbs 20:28)*

Don't expect to enjoy the cream of life if you keep your milk of human kindness all bottled up.

Hatred and anger are powerless when met with kindness.

Let me be a little kinder,
Let me be a little blinder
To the faults of those around me.   —*Edgar A. Guest*

Money will buy a fine dog, but only kindness makes him wag his tail.

Be kind to everybody. You never know who might show up on the jury at your trial.

Your own soul is nourished when you are kind; it is destroyed when you are cruel.
>   —*Solomon (Proverbs 11:17)*

He who is kind to his wife is kind to himself.

The person who sows seeds of kindness will have a perpetual harvest.

Better a little kindness while living than an extravagant floral display at the funeral.

If you treat your friend shabbily while he lives, you have no right to try to even up matters by whining over him when he is dead.   —*Joseph F. Berry*

Kindness is a language which the deaf can hear and the blind can see.

If someone were to pay you ten cents for every kind word you ever spoke about others and collect five cents for every unkind word, would you be rich or poor?

Kindness is the oil that takes the friction out of life.

Do not ask me to be kind; just ask me to act as though I were.   —*Jules Renard*

A kind word picks a man up when trouble weighs him down.

A kind heart is a fountain of gladness, making everything in its vicinity freshen into smiles.
                                                —*Washington Irving*

'Twas a thief said the last kind word to Christ: Christ took the kindness and forgave the theft.
                                                —*Robert Browning*

A man can pay back the loan of gold, but he dies forever in debt to those who are kind.

Never forget to be truthful and kind. Hold these virtues tightly. Write them deep within your heart.
                                                —*Solomon (Proverbs 3:3,4)*

Kindness makes a fellow feel good whether it's being done to him or by him.   —*Frank A. Clark*

One kind word can warm three winter months.
                                                —*Japanese proverb*

Kindness has converted more sinners than zeal, eloquence or learning.   —*Frederick W. Faber*

Be kind to people until you make your first million. After that, people will be kind to you.

A kindness put off until tomorrow may become only a bitter regret.

Never part without kind words. They might be your last.

Kindness is a warm breeze in a frigid climate, a radiant heat that melts the icebergs of fear, distrust and unhappiness.

Human kindness has never weakened the stamina or softened the fiber of a free people. A nation does not have to be cruel to be tough.   —*Franklin D. Roosevelt*

Be kind to unkind people—they need it the most.

Life is short, and we have never too much time for gladdening the hearts of those who are traveling the dark journey with us. Oh, be swift to love, make haste to be kind!   —*Henri-Frederic Amiel*

A kind word is better than a handout.

Life

The clock of life is wound but once,
And no man has the power
To tell when the hands will stop,
At late or early hour.
To lose one's health is sad indeed;
To lose one's soul is such a loss
That no man can restore.

1. Never put off till tomorrow what you can do today.
2. Never trouble another for what you can do yourself.
3. Never spend your money before you have it.
4. Never buy what you do not want just because it is cheap; it will be dear to you.
5. Pride costs us more than hunger, thirst or cold.
6. We never repent of having eaten too little.
7. Nothing is troublesome that we do willingly.
8. How much pain have cost us the evils which have never happened.
9. Take things always by their smooth handle.
10. When angry, count ten before you speak; if very angry, a hundred.
                                          —*Thomas Jefferson*

It wasn't until quite late in life that I discovered how easy it is to say, "I don't know."

—*Somerset Maugham*

My grandfather always said that living is like licking honey off a thorn.

—*Louis Adamic*

Most of the shadows of this life are caused by standing in one's own sunshine.

—*Ralph Waldo Emerson*

The Tide
There is a tide in the affairs of men
Which taken at the flood, leads on to fortune;
Omitted, all the voyage of their life,
Is bound in shallows and in miseries.

—*William Shakespeare*

Ten Spiritual Tonics
1. *Stop Worrying.* Worry kills life.
2. *Begin each day with a prayer.* It will arm your soul.
3. *Control appetite.* Overindulgence clogs body and mind.
4. *Accept your limitations.* All of us can't be great.
5. *Don't envy.* It wastes time and energy.
6. *Have faith in people.* Cynicism sours the disposition.
7. *Find a hobby.* It will relax your nerves.

8. *Read a book a week* to stimulate imagination and broaden your view.
9. *Spend some time alone,* for the peace of solitude and silence.
10. *Try to want what you have,* instead of spending your strength trying to get what you want.

—*Abraham L. Feinberg*

Pauses

In our whole-life melody, the music is broken off here and there by rests, and we foolishly think we have come to the end of time. God sends a time of forced leisure, a time of sickness and disappointed plans, and makes a sudden pause in the hymns of our lives, and we lament that our voice must be silent and our part missing in the music which ever goes up to the ear of our Creator. Not without design does God write the music of our lives. Be it ours to learn the time and not be dismayed at the rests. If we look up, God will beat the time for us.   —*John Ruskin*

Let us endeavor so to live that when we come to die even the undertaker will be sorry.   —*Mark Twain*

Religion can offer a man a burial service, but Christ offers every man new, abundant and everlasting life.

—*Wilma Reed*

May You Have
Enough happiness to keep you sweet;
Enough trials to keep you strong;
Enough sorrow to keep you human;
Enough hope to keep you happy;
Enough failure to keep you humble;
Enough success to keep you eager;
Enough friends to give you comfort;
Enough wealth to meet your needs;
Enough enthusiasm to look forward;
Enough faith to banish depression;
Enough determination to make each day
    better than yesterday.

The lowest ebb is the turn of the tide.
                    —Henry Wadsworth Longfellow

If I can stop one heart from breaking,
I shall not live in vain;
If I can ease one life the aching,
Or cool one pain,
Or help one fainting robin
Unto his nest again,
I shall not live in vain.   *—Emily Dickinson*

Life can only be understood backward; it must be
lived forward.   *—Søren Kierkegaard*

The Arrow and the Song
I shot an arrow into the air,
It fell to earth, I knew not where;
For, so swiftly it flew, the sight
Could not follow it in its flight.

I breathed a song into the air,
It fell to earth, I knew not where;
For who has sight so keen and strong,
That it can follow the flight of a song?

Long, long afterward, in an oak
I found the arrow, still unbroke;
And the song, from beginning to end,
I found again in the heart of a friend.
                    —*Henry Wadsworth Longfellow*

Life is a long lesson in humility.   —*James M. Barrie*

That best portion of a good man's life:
His little, nameless, unremembered acts
of kindness and of love.   —*William Wordsworth*

Life's a voyage that's homeward bound.
                    —*Herman Melville*

Life's greatest tragedy is to lose God and not to miss
Him.   —*F. W. Norwood*

My Task
To love someone more dearly ev'ry day,
To help a wandering child to find his way,
To ponder o'er a noble thought, and pray,
And smile when evening falls.
This is my task.

To follow truth as blind men long for light,
To do my best from dawn of day till night,
To keep my heart fit for His holy sight,
And answer when He calls.
This is my task.   *—Maude Louise Ray*

Listening

A wise old owl lived in an oak;
The more he saw, the less he spoke;
The less he spoke, the more he heard;
Why can't we all be like that bird?

We have two ears and only one tongue in order that
we may hear more and speak less.   *—Diogenes*

It's easy to entertain some people. All you have to do
is sit down and listen.

A good listener is not only popular everywhere, but after a while he knows something.   —*Wilson Mizner*

No man ever listened himself out of a job.
                                          —*Calvin Coolidge*

Once a man learns how to listen, he and his wife can remain on speaking terms indefinitely.

Half an hour's listening is essential except when you are very busy. Then a full hour is needed.
                                          —*St. Francis de Sales*

It is important for a good manager to know how to listen as well as to talk. We too often forget that communication is an exchange.   —*Lee Iacocca*

Formula for handling people:
1. Listen to the other person's story.
2. Listen to the other person's full story.
3. Listen to the other person's story first.
                                          —*General George Marshall*

A winner listens; a loser can't wait until it's his turn to talk.

From listening comes wisdom, and from speaking, repentance.   —*Italian proverb*

It takes courage to stand up and speak, as well as to sit down and listen.

Give every man thy ear, but few thy voice.
—William Shakespeare

The one who listens is the one who understands.

Husband, calling his wife to the phone: "Dear, someone wants to listen to you."

Too many of us have not learned to listen. Poor listeners range all the way from the impatient type— "That's nothing, wait'll you hear what I've done!" —to the person so absorbed in his own thoughts that he is not aware that someone has spoken. Learning to listen actively, and constructively, is as important as learning to speak, if communication is to be effective. *—William S. Tacey*

Nothing makes a person such a good listener as eavesdropping. *—Franklin P. Jones*

One of the best ways to persuade others is by listening to them. *—Dean Rusk*

The first step to wisdom is silence; the second is listening.

There are two kinds of bores—those who talk too
much and those who listen too little.

You can win more friends with your ears than with
your mouth.

A fool thinks he needs no advice, but a wise man
listens to others.   —*Solomon (Proverbs 12:15)*

I have no voice for singing;
I cannot make a speech;
I have no gift for music,
I know I cannot teach.

I am no good at leading;
I cannot "organize,"
And anything that I would write
Would never win a prize.

It seems my only talent
Is neither big nor rare—
Just to listen and encourage,
And to fill a vacant chair.

God still speaks to those who take the time to listen.

Love

The Love of God

There is an ocean—cold water without motion. In this ocean, however, is the Gulf Stream, hot water flowing from the equator toward the Pole. Inquire of all scientists how it is physically imaginable that a stream of hot water flows between the waters of the ocean which, so to speak, form its banks, the moving within the motionless, the hot within the cold. No scientist can explain it. Similarly, there is the God of love within the God of the forces of the universe— one with him, and yet so totally different. We let ourselves be seized and carried away by that vital stream.   —*Albert Schweitzer*

He loves each one of us, as if there were only one of us.   —*St. Augustine*

Thou shalt love the LORD thy God with all thine heart, and with all thy soul, and with all thy might.
                                    —*Deuteronomy 6:5 (KJV)*

God's love elevates us without inflating us, and humbles us without degrading us.   —*B. Nottage*

Indifference, not hate, is the strongest enemy of love.
                                        —*C. S. Lewis*

To love someone is to seek his or her best and
highest good.

Let love be your greatest aim.
                    —*The Apostle Paul (1 Corinthians 14:1)*

Love God completely; love others compassionately;
love yourself correctly.

Love one another; as I have loved you, that ye also
love one another.   —*Jesus (John 13:34, KJV)*

Someday, after we have mastered the air, the winds,
the tides and gravity, we will harness for God the
energies of love. And then, for the second time in the
history of the world, man will have discovered fire.
                                —*Teilhard de Chardin*

I have learned that only two things are necessary to
keep one's wife happy. First, let her think she is
having her way. And second, let her have it.
                                —*Lyndon B. Johnson*

Love—what you keep to yourself you lose, what you
give away you keep forever.

Love is the basic need of human nature, for without it, life is disrupted emotionally, mentally, spiritually and physically. —*Dr. Karl Menninger*

Greater love hath no man than this, that a man lay down his life for his friends. —*Jesus (John 15:13, KJV)*

Love is the feeling that makes a woman make a man make a fool of himself.

Life is just one fool thing after another; love is just two fool things after each other.

When love and skill work together, expect a masterpiece. —*Charles Reade*

Love without return is like a question without an answer.

'Tis better to have loved and lost
Than never to have loved at all.
—*Alfred, Lord Tennyson*

Hatred stirs old quarrels, but love overlooks insults.
—*Solomon (Proverbs 10:12)*

Love cures people—both the ones who give it and the ones who receive it. —*Karl Menninger*

And love in the heart wasn't put there to stay; Love isn't love 'till you give it away.
—*Oscar Hammerstein II*

Money can build a house, but it takes love to make it a home.

Love your enemies.   —*Jesus (Matthew 5:44, KJV)*

A husband knows his wife loves him when she returns a dress he can't afford.

Don't underestimate love at first sight. Many of us might not pass a second inspection.

Love is a fabric which never fades, no matter how often it is washed in the waters of adversity and grief.

Love forgets mistakes; nagging about them parts the best of friends.   —*Solomon (Proverbs 17:9)*

Faults are thick where love is thin.   —*James Howell*

Sign in an airline's office: "God loves you and I'm trying."

You can give without loving, but you cannot love without giving.   —*Amy Carmichael*

He drew a circle that shut me out—
Heretic, rebel, a thing to flout.
But love and I had the wit to win:
We drew a circle that took him in.   *—Edwin Markham*

Love is a form of insanity which makes a girl marry
her boss and work for him the rest of her life without
salary.

Love makes the lonelies go away.

Love begins when a person feels another person's
needs to be as important as his own.
—Harry S. Sullivan

He who falls in love with himself will have no rivals.

Hallmarks of True Love
  1. A genuine interest in the other person and all
     that he or she says or does.
  2. A community of tastes, ideals, and standards
     with no serious clashes.
  3. A greater happiness in being with the one person
     than with any other.
  4. A real unhappiness when the other person is
     absent.
  5. A great feeling of comradeship.

6. A willingness to give and take.
7. A pride in the other person when comparisons
   are made.   —*Newell W. Edson*

Love is giving freely, expecting nothing in return.
Law concerns itself with an equitable exchange, *this
for that*. Law is made necessary by people; love is
made possible by God.   —*Mary Carson*

Loyalty
(also Patriotism)

There is one element that is worth its weight in gold
and that is loyalty. It will cover a multitude of weak-
nesses.   —*Philip Armour*

Loyalty is one thing a leader cannot do without. It is
as priceless as it is rare. It creates a quiet confidence
in the heart of any leader and is the assurance of success in any enterprise.   —*A. P. Gouthey*

Those who expect to reap the blessings of freedom
must, like men, undergo the fatigue of supporting it.
                                     —*Thomas Paine*

If you are ashamed to stand by your colors, you had better seek another flag.

To have no loyalty is to have no dignity and in the end no manhood.   —*Peter T. Forsyth*

You cannot serve two masters: God and money. For you will hate one and love the other, or else the other way around.   —*Jesus (Matthew 6:24)*

Today's version of a loyal patriot is the man who is sincerely sorry that he has but one income to give to his country.

In the evening of my memory I come back to West Point. Always there echoes and re-echoes: duty, honor, country.   —*Douglas MacArthur*

Loyalty is being true to someone on top.

I am glad to see that pride in our country and its accomplishments is not a thing of the past. I still get a hard-to-define feeling when the flag goes up, and I know you do, too. Let us hope that none of us loses that feeling. As our knowledge of the universe increases, may God grant us the wisdom and guidance to use it wisely.   —*John H. Glenn*

A true and loyal patriot is the fellow who is always ready and willing to lay down your life for his country.

Lack of loyalty and patriotism is one of the major causes of failure in every walk of life. —*Napoleon Hill*

We must all hang together, or assuredly we shall all hang separately.   —*Benjamin Franklin*

Patriotism is the pain in the neck you feel when a foreigner wins the championship.

The sum of the whole matter is this: If our civilization is to survive materially, it must be redeemed spiritually.   —*Woodrow Wilson*

Not for the flag
Of any land because myself was born there
Will I give up my life.
But I will love that land where man is free,
And that will I defend.   —*Edna St. Vincent Millay*

If you work for a man, for heaven's sake, work for him.   —*Kin Hubbard*

Loyalty to petrified opinion never yet broke a chain or freed a human soul.

Loyalty: sticking with your husband through all the trouble he wouldn't have had if he hadn't married you.

When young, we are faithful to individuals; when older, we grow more loyal to situations and to types.
                                        —*Cyril Connolly*

We are all in the same boat in a stormy sea, and we owe each other a terrible loyalty.   —*G. K. Chesterton*

Motivation

Desire is the key to motivation, but it's the determination and commitment to an unrelenting pursuit of your goal—a commitment to excellence—that will enable you to attain the success you seek.
                                        —*Mario Andretti*

We can justify our every deed but God looks at our motives.   —*Solomon (Proverbs 21:2)*

We know nothing about motivation. All we can do is write books about it.   —*Peter Drucker*

Coaches who can outline plays on a black board are
a dime a dozen. The ones who win get inside their
players and motivate.   —*Vince Lombardi*

Awareness
God—let me be aware.
Let me not stumble blindly down the ways,
Just getting somehow safely through the days,
Not even groping for another hand,
Not even wondering why it was all planned,
Eyes to the ground unseeking for the light,
Soul never aching for a wild-winged flight,
Please, keep me eager just to do my share.
God—let me be aware.

God—let me be aware.
Stab my soul fiercely with others' pain,
Let me walk seeing horror and stain.
Let my hands, groping, find other hands.
Give me the heart that divines, understands.
Give me the courage, wounded, to fight.
Flood me with knowledge, drench me in light.
Please, keep me eager just to do my share.
God—let me be aware.   —*Miriam Teichner*

We do not evangelize because we expect results. We
evangelize because we are sent men.
                                   —*Joseph D. Blinco*

Six-thirty is my time to rise,
But I'm seldom bright of eye;
Part of me says, "Look alive!"
And the other part asks, "Why?"

The biggest gap in the world is the gap between the
justice of a cause and the motives of the people
pushing it.   —*John P. Grier*

Father: "Eat your dinner!"
Child: "Motivate me!"

If no action is to be deemed virtuous for which
malice can imagine a sinister motive, then there was
never a virtuous action; no, not even in the life of our
Savior Himself. But He has taught us to judge the
tree by its fruit, and to leave motives to Him who can
alone see into them.   —*Thomas Jefferson*

Whatever you do, work at it with all your heart, as
working for the Lord, not for men.
                      —*The Apostle Paul (Colossians 3:23, NIV)*

In winter, the big problem is motivation—how to get
72 inches of son to shovel 3½ inches of snow.

The noblest motive is the public good.   —*Virgil*

One motivation is worth ten threats, two pressures
and six reminders.   —*Paul Sweeney*

Do your best to present yourself to God as one
approved.   —*The Apostle Paul (2 Timothy 2:15, NIV)*

In the course of development relatively stable units
of personality gradually emerge. Such units are
always the product of the two central and vital func-
tions of mental life: motivation and organization.
Motivation refers to the "go" of mental life, organization to its patterning.   —*Gordon W. Allport*

Motivation is what gets you started. Habit is what
keeps you going.   —*Jim Ryun*

People are always motivated for at least two reasons:
The one they tell you about, and a secret one.
                                     —*O. A. Battista*

Motives are invisible but they are the true test of
character.   —*Alfred A. Montapert*

It is motive alone that gives character to the actions
of men.   —*Jean De La Bruyere*

Never ascribe to an opponent motives meaner than
your own.   —*James M. Barrie*

We would often be ashamed of our best actions if
the world only knew the motives behind them.
—*Francois de La Rochefoucauld*

He that does good for God's sake seeks neither praise
nor reward, but he is sure of both in the end.
—*William Penn*

Optimism/Pessimism

An optimist is a person who
is a hope addict;
lets his insurance lapse;
doesn't know what's coming to him;
always opts to look on the bright side of things;
marries his secretary thinking that he'll continue to
    dictate to her;
when he can't be thankful for what he has, is thank-
    ful for what he has escaped;
looks at an oyster and expects a pearl; the pessimist
    expects ptomaine poisoning;
counts his blessings while the pessimist discounts his;
starts putting on her shoes when the preacher says,
    "And now in conclusion . . . ";

has no brakes; the pessimist has no motor;
hurries because he thinks his date is ready and wait-
    ing for him.

A pessimist is a person who
believes that life is neither worth living nor leaving;
cannot enjoy his health today because he may be
    sick tomorrow;
believes that the only dreams that come true are the
    nightmares;
not only expects the worst but makes the worst of it
    when it happens;
does not see the whole of the donut, but sees only
    the hole *in* the donut;
doesn't expect to get what he wants, but expects to
    be disappointed if he does;
believes that the future is not what it used to be;
is convinced that the chief purpose of sunshine is to
    cast shadows;
forgets his blessings but remembers his troubles.

Optimism: the doctrine or belief that everything is
beautiful, including what is ugly, everything good,
especially the bad, and everything right that is wrong.
                                            —*Ambrose Bierce*

An opportunist pulls himself up by *your* bootstraps.
                                            —*Al Bernstein*

Somebody said that it couldn't be done—
    But he with a chuckle replied
That maybe it couldn't but he would be one
    Who wouldn't say so till he'd tried.

So he buckled right in, with a bit of a grin
    On his face—if he worried he hid it;
He started to sing, as he tackled the thing
    That couldn't be done—and he did it!

Somebody scoffed, "Oh, you'll never do that—
    At least no one has ever done it";
But he took off his coat and he took off his hat,
    And the first thing we knew, he'd begun it.

With a lift of his chin, and a bit of a grin
    Without any doubting or "quit it,"
He started to sing, as he tackled the thing
    That couldn't be done, and he did it!
                                        —*Edgar Guest*

I told him, "Son, I can't understand it with you. Is it
ignorance or apathy?"

He said, "Coach, I don't know and I don't care."
                                        —*Frank Layden*

When confronted with a Goliath-size problem,
which way do you respond: "He's too big to hit," or,
like David, "He's too big to miss"?

He who sees an enemy behind every tree is a pessimist.

The wicked flee when no one is chasing them! But the godly are bold as lions!   —*Solomon (Proverbs 28:1)*

Optimists are nostalgic about the future.

A pessimist looks at the world through woes-colored glasses.

An optimist is a fellow who believes a housefly is looking for a way to get out.   —*George Nathan*

A hopeless pessimist is always building dungeons in the air.

A pessimist is someone who feels bad when he feels good for fear he'll feel worse when he feels better.
                                        —*Thomas Jefferson*

[Optimism] is the mania of maintaining that everything is well when we are wretched.   —*Voltaire*

Everybody, my friend, everybody lives for something better to come. That's why we want to be considerate of every man. Who knows what's in him, why he was born and what he can do?   —*Maxim Gorky*

Some people are making such thorough plans for
rainy days that they aren't enjoying today's sunshine.
                                    —*William Feather*

Pessimists always take the cynic route.
                                    —*Antoni Tabok*

No matter how bright the sunshine, pious pessimists
point to the tunnel at the end of the light.

The pessimist sees the difficulty in every opportunity;
the optimist sees the opportunity in every difficulty.
                                    —*L. P. Jacks*

A pessimist thinks everybody is as nasty as himself,
and hates them for it.

A pessimist says that any time things appear to be
going better, you have overlooked something.

The optimist proclaims that we live in the best of all
possible worlds, and the pessimist fears this is true.
                                    —*James Branch Cabell*

Because you have occasional low spells of despon-
dency, don't despair. The sun has a sinking spell
every night but it rises again all right the next
morning.   —*Henry Van Dyke*

Optimism is
taking a camera along when you go fishing;
the ability to smile at misfortune when fortune
    doesn't smile at you;
expecting your wife to drive a car six feet wide
    through a garage doorway eight feet narrow;
never worrying about the future because it never
    becomes serious until it is the present;
the cheerful frame of mind that enables a teapot to
    sing, though it is in hot water up to its nose.

A pessimist is a person who
is always good for bad news;
is never happy unless he's miserable;
burns his bridges before he gets to them.

A pessimist says his glass is already half empty. An
optimist says his glass is still half full.

You know it's going to be a bad week when your
boss mails you want ads.

A pessimist is a man who has been compelled to live
with an optimist.   —*Elbert Hubbard*

An optimist is a driver who thinks that that empty
space at the curb won't have a hydrant beside it.

A pessimist always looks both ways when he crosses a one-way street.

Always borrow from a pessimist; he never expects to get it back.

A pessimist says the lily belongs to the onion family; an optimist declares that the onion belongs to the lily family.

An optimist is one who makes the best of it when he gets the worst of it.

Pessimist: one who, when he has a choice of two evils, chooses both.   *—Oscar Wilde*

A pessimist is an optimist who thought he could buy something for a dollar.

The year's at the spring
And day's at the morn;
Morning's at seven;
The hillside's dew-pearled;
The lark's on the wing;
The snail's on the thorn;
God's in His heaven—
All's right with the world.   *—Robert Browning*

The future is as bright as the promises of God.
—*Adoniram Judson*

Patience

Patience is the ability to count down before blasting off.

If you are patient in one moment of anger, you will escape a hundred days of sorrow.   —*Chinese proverb*

Adopt the pace of nature: Her secret is patience.
—*Ralph Waldo Emerson*

The horn of plenty is the one the guy behind you has on his car.   —*Crane*

Is your life full of difficulties and temptations? Then be happy, for when the way is rough, your patience has a chance to grow. So let it grow, and don't try to squirm out of your problems. For when your patience is finally in full bloom, then you will be ready for anything, strong in character, full and complete.   —*James (1:2–4)*

Child's definition of impatience: waiting in a hurry.

Don't borrow trouble. Be patient and you'll have enough of your own.

Be glad for all God is planning for you. Be patient in trouble, and prayerful always.
—*The Apostle Paul (Romans 12:12)*

All things come round to him who will but wait.
—*Henry W. Longfellow*

Never a tear bedims the eye that time and patience will not dry.   —*Harte*

All things come to him who waits, provided he knows what he is waiting for.   —*Woodrow Wilson*

They praised me for being so patient,
I smiled and I waited, that's true.
But my waiting was not really patience,
I just didn't know what to do!   —*Dwayne W. Laws*

Be patient when a person growls at you; he may be living with a bear!

Patience is a quality you admire in the driver behind you and scorn in the one ahead.

Patience is a virtue that carries a lot of wait.

Bean by bean the bag is filled.

Patience is the companion of wisdom.

Living would be easier if men showed as much patience at home as they do when they're fishing.

I wanted to be a doctor, but I didn't have any patience.

Some people pray, "Lord, give me patience, and I want it *right now!*"   —*Bernard R. DeRemer*

Patience: a bitter plant that produces sweet fruit.

Impatient people always get there too late.
                                              —*Jean Dutourd*

You must have patience on a diet—especially if it's your wife who's on it.

Sign in a Texas country store: "Be patient. None of us am perfect."

You never realize how patient you can be until the fellow who is arguing with you is your boss.

Like farmers, we need to learn that we can't sow and reap the same day.

Patience and diligence, like faith, move mountains.
—*William Penn*

They also serve who only stand and wait.
—*John Milton*

No road is too long for the man who advances deliberately and without haste; and no honors are too distant for the man who prepares himself for them with patience. —*Bruyere*

Peace

If there is righteousness in the heart, there will be beauty in the character. If there be beauty in the character, there will be harmony in the home. If there is harmony in the home, there will be order in the nation. When there is order in the nation, there will be peace in the world. —*Chinese proverb*

Sign in Southern psychiatrist's office: Y'all calm!

Thou wilt keep him in perfect peace, whose mind is stayed on thee: because he trusteth in thee.
—*Isaiah (26:3, KJV)*

The amazing thing about a man being arrested for disturbing the peace these days is that he could find any.

Keeping peace in the family requires patience, love, understanding—and at least two television sets.

The best way for a housewife to have a few peaceful moments to herself at the close of the day is to start doing the dishes.

Peace is the luxury you enjoy between your children's bedtime and your own.   —*Lester D. Klimek*

A dry crust eaten in peace is better than steak every day along with argument and strife.
—*Solomon (Proverbs 17:1)*

All men desire peace, but very few desire those things that make for peace.   —*Thomas á Kempis*

For the maintenance of peace, nations should avoid the pin pricks which forerun cannon shots.
—*Napoleon*

When at night you cannot sleep,
talk to the Shepherd and stop counting sheep.

At the heart of the cyclone
tearing the sky,
And flinging the clouds and towers by,
Is a place of central calm;
And so in the roar of mortal things,
There is a place where my spirit sings,
In the hollow of God's palm.   —*Edwin Markham*

But all who listen to me shall live in peace and safety,
unafraid.   —*Solomon (Proverbs 1:33)*

Said the robin to the sparrow,
I should really like to know
Why these anxious human beings
Rush around and worry so.

Said the sparrow to the robin,
Friend, I think that it must be
That they have no heavenly Father
Such as cares for you and me.

What the world needs is peace that passes all
misunderstanding.

No God, no peace; know God, know peace.

There will be no peace as long as God remains
unseated at the conference table.

The Bible teaches us that there is no foundation for
enduring peace on earth, except in righteousness;
that it is our duty to suffer for that cause if need be;
that we are bound to fight for it if we have the
power; and that if God gives us the victory we must
use it for the perpetuation of righteous peace.
                                          —*Henry Van Dyke*

Three enemies of personal peace: regrets over
yesterday's mistakes, anxiety over tomorrow's
problems, and ingratitude for today's blessings.
                                          —*William A. Ward*

The only time I find peace is when I stop looking
for it.

Peace cannot be kept by force. It can only be
achieved by understanding.   —*Albert Einstein*

Blessed are the peacemakers: for they shall be called
the children of God.   —*Jesus (Matthew 5:9, KJV)*

Peace, like charity, begins at home.
                                          —*Franklin D. Roosevelt*

Have courage for the great sorrows of life and
patience for the small ones; and when you have
laboriously accomplished your daily task, go to sleep
in peace. God is awake.   *—Victor Hugo*

Persistence

So, my dear brothers, since future victory is sure, be
strong and steady, always abounding in the Lord's
work, for you know that nothing you do for the Lord
is ever wasted as it would be if there were no resur-
rection.   *—The Apostle Paul (1 Corinthians 15:58)*

When nothing seems to help, I go and look at a
stonecutter hammering away at his rock perhaps a
hundred times without as much as a crack showing
in it.

Yet at the hundred and first blow it will split in two,
and I know it was not that blow that did it—but all
that had gone before.   *—Jacob Riis*

No one would have ever crossed the ocean if he
could have gotten off the ship in a storm.
    —Charles Kettering

A Poet's Proverb
God's road is all uphill,
But do not tire,
Rejoice that we may still
Keep climbing higher.   —*Arthur Guiterman*

We are judged by what we finish, not by what we start.

True Rest
Rest is not quitting
The busy career;
Rest is the fitting
Of self to one's sphere.

'Tis the brook's motion
Clear without strife,
Fleeting to ocean,
After his life.

'Tis loving and serving,
The highest and best;
'Tis onward, unswerving,
And this is true rest.   —*Johann Wolfgang Von Goethe*

Persistent people begin their success where others end in failure.

Failure is the path of least persistence.

He who stops at third base to congratulate himself will never score a home run.

The game isn't over till it's over.
—*Lawrence Peter "Yogi" Berra*

Wealthy people miss one of life's greatest pleasures—making the last payment.

The next mile is the only one a person really has to make. —*Danish proverb*

I'm a slow walker, but I never walk back.
—*Abraham Lincoln*

If you can consistently do your best, the worst won't happen. —*B. C. Forbes*

Nothing in the world can take the place of persistence. Talent will not; nothing is more common than unsuccessful men with talent. Genius will not; unrewarded genius is almost a proverb.

Education will not; the world is full of educated derelicts.

Persistence and determination alone are omnipotent.
—*Calvin Coolidge*

There is no poverty that can overtake diligence.
                                        —*Japanese proverb*

By perseverance, the snail reached the Ark.
                                        —*Charles Spurgeon*

A diamond is a chunk of coal that stuck to its job.

I hold a doctrine to which I owe much, indeed, but
all the little I ever had, namely, that with ordinary
talent and extraordinary perseverance all things are
attainable.   —*T. F. Buxton*

He who starts many things finishes nothing.

Life is hard,
By the yard;
But by the inch,
Life's a cinch!   —*Jean L. Gordon*

When William Carey was asked the reason for his
success as a missionary, he replied, "I can plod."

We conquer—not in any brilliant fashion—we
conquer by continuing.   —*George Matheson*

The man who removes a mountain begins by
carrying away small stones.   —*Chinese proverb*

Do all the good you can,
By all the means you can,
In all the ways you can,
In all the places you can,
At all the times you can,
To all the people you can,
As long as ever you can.　　　　*—John Wesley*

Consider the postage stamp: its usefulness consists in the ability to stick to one thing till it gets there.
　　　　—Josh Billings

He who has made a start has half the job done.

Stopping at third base adds no more to the score than striking out.

Stick to your job until one of you is through.

Better the shoulder to the wheel than the back to the wall.

Perseverance has been defined as sticking to something you're not stuck on.

It's often the last key on the ring that opens the door.

Paralyze resistance with persistence.　　*—Woody Hayes*

Perseverance is the result of a strong will. Obstinacy is the result of a strong "won't."

Our greatest glory is not in never failing, but in rising every time we fall.

The road to success runs uphill, so don't expect to break any speed records.

The secret of success is to start from scratch and keep on scratching.

Our greatest weakness lies in giving up. The most certain way to succeed is always to try one more time.
                                                     —*Thomas Edison*

It is my belief that talent is plentiful, and that what is lacking is staying power.   —*Doris Lessing*

When you repress or suppress these things which you don't want to live with, you don't really solve the problem because you don't bury the problem dead—you bury it alive and active within you.
                                                     —*John Powell*

Prayer

Amen

This little word has entered more languages (perhaps over 1000) than any other single word in human speech. How that came to be is a fascinating story. It is said that in Alexandria, Egypt, around 250 B.C.E., King Ptolemy desired a translation of the Hebrew Bible. He set 70 or 72 scholars, chosen from the Jewish community, to work on the translation. They reached the word "Amen," first cousin of *Emet* (truth). "Amen" meant "So be it"; or, "May this prayer come true." There was no single Greek word expressing this thought, so they turned it into a Greek word—"Amen." When the Bible was translated into Latin, "Amen" became a Latin word. And so it went.

A hundred times a day I remind myself that my inner and outer life depend on the labors of other men, living and dead, and that I must exert myself in order to give in the same measure as I have received and am still receiving.   *—Albert Einstein*

Life is fragile—handle with prayer.

In the morning, prayer is the key that opens to us the treasures of God's mercies and blessings; in the evening, it is the key that shuts us up under his protection and safeguard.

The less I pray, the harder it gets; the more I pray, the better it goes.   —*Martin Luther*

Prayer
Lord, what a change within us one short hour
Spent in thy presence will prevail to make!
What heavy burdens from our bosoms take,
What parched grounds refresh as with a shower!
We kneel, and all around us seems to lower;
We rise, and all, the distant and the near,
Stands forth in sunny outline brave and clear;
We kneel, how weak! we rise, how full of power!
Why, therefore, should we do ourselves this wrong,
Or others, that we are not always strong,
That we are ever overborne with care,
That we should ever weak or heartless be,
Anxious or troubled, when with us is prayer,
And joy and strength and courage are with thee!
                        —*Richard Chenevix Trench*

Who goes to bed and does not pray, maketh two
nights to every day.   —*George Herbert*

If two of you shall agree on earth as to anything that they shall ask, it shall be done for them of my Father which is in heaven.   *—Jesus (Matthew 18:19)*

Lord, make me a channel of thy peace
That where there is hatred I may bring love,
That where there is wrong I may bring the spirit of
 forgiveness,
That where there is discord I may bring harmony,
That where there is error I may bring truth,
That where there is doubt I may bring faith,
That where there is despair I may bring hope,
That where there are shadows I may bring thy light,
That where there is sadness I may bring joy.
Lord, grant that I may seek rather
To comfort—than to be comforted;
To understand—than to be understood;
To love—than to be loved;
For it is by giving that one receives;
It is by self-forgetting that one finds;
It is by forgiving that one is forgiven;
It is by dying that one awakens to eternal life.
     —St. Frances of Assisi

Notice on high school bulletin board: "In the event of nuclear attack, all bans on prayer on this campus will be lifted."

A prayer in its simplest definition is merely a wish
turned Godward.   —*Phillips Brooks*

Prayer is the contemplation of the facts of life from
the highest point of view.   —*Ralph Waldo Emerson*

There will always be prayer in public schools—as
long as there are final exams to take.
                                   —*B. Norman Frisch*

If your day is hemmed with prayer, it is less likely to
unravel.

Two small boys were sitting in the corner facing the
wall. "What are you here for?" one asked.
"I got caught talking to Joe! And you?"
"I got caught talking to God!"

Do not pray for easy lives. Pray to be stronger men.
Do not pray for tasks commensurate with your
strength. Pray for strength commensurate with your
tasks.   —*Phillips Brooks*

Now there's even a "dial-a-prayer" for atheists. You
call a number and nobody answers.

What isn't won in prayer first, is never won at all.
                                   —*Malcolm Cronk*

The Lord hates the gifts of the wicked, but delights in the prayers of his people. —*Solomon (Proverbs 15:8)*

If God shuts one door, He opens another.
—*Irish proverb*

The Lord is far from the wicked, but he hears the prayers of the righteous. —*Solomon (Proverbs 15:29)*

Man is never so tall as when he kneels before God— never so great as when he humbles himself before God. And the man who kneels to God can stand up to anything. —*Louis H. Evans*

At the close of a catechetical class, a twelve-year-old girl was called on to pray. Said she, "O Lord, thank You for all You've done, and keep up the good work."

Prayer is the key of the morning and the bolt of the night.

Every step in the progress of missions is directly traceable to prayer. It has been the preparation for every new triumph and the secret of all success.
—*A. T. Pierson*

Many prayers go to the dead letter office of heaven for want of sufficient direction.

Why Wonder?
If radio's slim fingers
can pluck a melody
From the night and toss it over
a continent or sea;
If the petalled white notes
of a violin
are blown across a mountain
or a city's din;
If songs, like crimson roses
are culled from the thin blue air;
Why should mortals wonder
that God hears and answers prayer?
                                        —Ethel Romig Fuller

Prayer doesn't get man's will done in heaven; it gets
God's will done on earth.   *—Ronald Dunn*

Preacher: "Do you say your prayers at night, little
boy?"

Jimmy: "Yes, sir."

Preacher: "Do you say your prayers in the morning,
too?"

Jimmy: "No, sir. I ain't scared in the daytime."

Prayer is the stop that keeps you going.

When praying, don't give God instructions. God listens to prayer, not advice.

Prayer is exhaling the spirit of man and inhaling the Spirit of God.   —*Edwin Keith*

He who cannot reach the mission field on his feet can reach it on his knees.

Prayer at its highest is a two-way conversation, and for me the most important part is listening to God's replies.   —*Frank Laubach*

Lord, fill my mouth
with worthwhile stuff,
And nudge me when
I've said enough!

A teenager's view of prayer: "There are four answers to prayer—yes, no, wait awhile, and you've got to be kidding!"

True prayer is a way of life, not just in case of an emergency.

We know that God does not listen to sinners. He listens to the godly man who does his will.
                                  —*John (9:31, NIV)*

Before we can pray, "Thy Kingdom come," we must
be willing to pray, "My kingdom go." —*Alan Redpath*

If God is your Father, please call home.

It's a good idea to tune your instruments by prayer
before the concert of the day begins.

Many a man kept going straight because his mother
bent her knees in prayer.

Let's move from theology to kneeology! Power for
victory in spiritual warfare is found in prayer.
—*Robert R. Lawrence*

Many a fellow is praying for rain with his tub the
wrong side up.

Don't pray to escape trouble. Don't pray to be comfortable in your emotions. Pray to do the will of God
in every situation. Nothing else is worth praying for.
—*Samuel M. Shoemaker*

The man who says his prayers in the evening is a
captain posting his sentries. After that, he can sleep.
—*Charles Baurdelaire*

He who is a stranger to prayer is a stranger to power.

When I pray, coincidences happen, and when I don't, they don't.
—*William Temple*

God does nothing but in answer to prayer.
—*John Wesley*

Many people pray as if God were a big aspirin pill. They come only when they hurt.
—*B. Graham Dienert*

Seven days without a prayer makes one weak.
—*Allen E. Bartlett*

I have discovered that prayer is the secret weapon of the kingdom of God. It is like a missile that can be fired toward any spot on earth, travel undetected at the speed of thought, and hit its target every time.
—*Ronald Dunn*

More things are wrought by prayer than this world dreams of.
—*Alfred, Lord Tennyson*

Ask, and it shall be given you; seek, and ye shall find; knock, and it shall be opened unto you.
—*Jesus (Matthew 7:7, KJV)*

I have found the greatest power in the world is the power of prayer.
—*Cecil B. DeMille*

Pray hardest when it is hardest to pray. Prayer is a powerful thing, for God has bound and tied Himself thereto.   —*Martin Luther*

He who spreads the sails of prayer will eventually fly the flag of praise.

The one concern of the devil is to keep Christians from praying. He fears nothing from prayerless studies, prayerless works and prayerless religion. He laughs at our toil, mocks at our wisdom, but trembles when we pray.   —*Samuel Chadwick*

Nothing lies beyond the reach of prayer except that which lies outside the will of God.

And this is the confidence that we have in him, that, if we ask anything according to his will, he heareth us.   —*John (1 John 5:14, KJV)*

I am better or worse as I pray more or less. It works for me with mathematical precision.
                                          —*E. Stanley Jones*

Prayer is not conquering God's reluctance, but taking hold of God's willingness.   —*Phillips Brooks*

Meeting minutes: "Rev. David B. Matthews presided, and opened and opened and opened and opened the meeting with prayer."

I have been driven to my knees many times by the overwhelming conviction that I had nowhere else to go. My own wisdom and that of all those about me seemed insufficient for that day.   —*Abraham Lincoln*

Prayer is the one approach that can transform drudgery into doxology.   —*William Vander Hoven*

He who is swept off his feet needs to get back on his knees.

He who runs from God in the morning will scarcely find Him the rest of the day.   —*John Bunyan*

When your day is hemmed with prayer it is less likely to unravel.

A Christian sees more on his knees than a philosopher on his tiptoes.

Pray to God, but row toward the shore.
     —*Russian proverb*

The great tragedy of life is not unanswered prayer,
but unoffered prayer.   —*Philip Melanchthon*

If I could hear Christ praying for me in the next
room, I would not fear a million enemies. Yet distance makes no difference. He is praying for me.
                                   —*Robert Murray McCheyne*

The reason you don't have what you want is that
you don't ask God for it.   —*James (4:2b)*

Behind every work of God you will always find
some kneeling form.   —*Dwight L. Moody*

A lot of kneeling keeps you in good standing with
God. If your knees are knocking, kneel on them.

Time spent in prayer will yield more than that given
to work. Prayer alone gives work its worth and its
success. Prayer opens the way for God Himself to do
His work in us and through us. Let our chief work as
God's messengers be intercession; in it we secure the
presence and power of God to go with us.
                                   —*Andrew Murray*

Preparation

Any enterprise is built by wise planning, becomes strong through common sense, and profits wonderfully by keeping abreast of the facts.
—Solomon (Proverbs 24:3,4)

We can make our plans, but the final outcome is in God's hands. *—Solomon (Proverbs 16:1)*

Failure to prepare is preparing to fail. *—John Wooden*

One of life's most painful moments comes when we must admit that we didn't do our homework, that we are not prepared. *—Merlin Olson*

He who doesn't know where he's going should not start his journey.

It is pleasant to see plans develop. That is why fools refuse to give them up even when they are wrong.
—Solomon (Proverbs 13:19)

Don't cross the bridge until you have the exact toll ready.

Luck is what happens when preparation meets
opportunity.   —*Elmer Letterman*

Make no little plans;
They have no magic to stir
    men's blood
And probably themselves will not
    be realized.
Make big plans; aim high
    in hope and work,
Remembering that a noble,
    logical diagram
Once recorded will not die.   —*David H. Burnham*

The time to repair the roof is when the sun is shining.
                                                —*John F. Kennedy*

The experience taught me to live your life every day
as if you're ready for it to be your last—to get your
ducks in a row.
                    —*Reba McEntire, following the deaths of
                        seven band members and her tour man-
                        ager in a plane crash March 16, 1991*

To be prepared for war is one of the most effectual
means of preserving peace.   —*George Washington*

These unhappy times call for the building of plans
... that build from the bottom up and not from the
top down, that put their faith once more in the for-
gotten man at the bottom of the economic pyramid.
—*Franklin D. Roosevelt*

Today's preparation determines tomorrow's
achievement.

Chance favors the prepared mind.   —*Louis Pasteur*

Successful salesmanship is 90% preparation and
10% presentation.

Priorities

In everything you do, put God first, and he will direct
you and crown your efforts with success.
—*Solomon (Proverbs 3:6)*

There are men so conservative they believe nothing
should be done for the first time.   —*Alexander Smith*

The first thing to do is fall in love with your work.

Show me the way
not to fortune and fame,
Not how to win laurels
or praise for my name—
But show me the way
to spread "The Great Story"
That Thine is The Kingdom
and Power and Glory.   —*Helen Steiner Rice*

Seek ye first the kingdom of God and His righteousness; and all these things shall be added unto you.
                            —*Jesus (Matthew 6:33, KJV)*

He who does not knot his thread will lose his first
stitch.

The first step to wisdom is to avoid the common
fallacy which considers everything profound that is
obscure.

Do not have your concert first and tune your instruments afterward. Begin the day with God.
                            —*James Hudson Taylor*

He who asks a question may be a fool for five minutes: he who never asks a question remains a fool
forever.

Wise men learn more from fools than fools from
wise men. —*Cato*

Asking saves a lot of guesswork.

People who want to move mountains must start by
carrying away small stones.

Only one life, 'twill soon be past.
Only what's done for Christ will last.

Honor the Lord by giving him the first part of all
your income, and he will fill your barns with wheat
and barley and overflow your wine vats with the
finest wines. —*Solomon (Proverbs 3:9,10)*

Taking first things first often reduces the most com-
plex human problem to a manageable proportion.
—*Dwight Eisenhower*

We are silent at the beginning of the day because
God should have the first word, and we are silent
before going to sleep because the last word also
belongs to God. —*Dietrich Bonhoeffer*

Problems

Problem solving: First, set down the problem to study it, to solve it. Second, collect all the facts. Third, study the facts, think about them. Fourth, get possible solutions from trial and error. Fifth, select the best possible solution from these.

—*William James*

Some people approach every problem with an open mouth.   —*Adlai Stevenson*

Why can't problems hit us when we're 17 and know everything?

In this Book will be found the solution of all the problems of the world.   —*Calvin Coolidge*

The best way to solve your own problem is to help someone else solve his.

Problems are only opportunities in work clothes.

—*Henry J. Kaiser*

Problems shouldn't be faced; they should be attacked.

A problem well stated is a problem half resolved.
—*Charles F. Kettering*

If a care is too small to be turned into a prayer, it is too small to be made into a burden.

So you've got a problem? That's good! Why? Because repeated victories over your problems are the rungs on your ladder to success. With each victory you grow in wisdom, stature and experience. You become a bigger, better, more successful person each time you meet a problem and tackle and conquer it with a positive mental attitude.   —*Clement Stone*

Be thankful for problems, for if they were less difficult, someone with less ability would have your job.

It's too bad human beings cannot exchange problems. Everyone knows how to solve the other fellow's.

Do yourself a favor when you have a personal or business problem: don't tell anyone. You see, 20 percent don't care, and 80 percent are glad to hear about it.

Every problem is a possibility in disguise.

God has no problems, only plans.   —*Corrie ten Boom*

For every problem God permits us to have, there is a
solution.   —*Thomas Edison*

Our problems should make us better not bitter.

The man who has no more problems to solve is out
of the game.   —*Elbert Hubbard*

Congress has figured out the right system. When its
members encounter a problem they can't solve, they
subsidize it.

We have to approach a problem with as much calm
and wisdom as we possess.   —*Nehru*

A harried housewife in Omaha sighed, "I have so
many problems that if something terrible happened
to me it would be at least two weeks before I could
get around to worrying about it."

The problem is that the key to success doesn't
always fit your ignition.

Part of the problem today is that we have a surplus of
simple answers, and a shortage of simple questions.

If you are not having problems, you are missing an
opportunity for growth.   —*Thomas Blandi*

Psychiatrists tell us that talking helps solve our problems—it often causes them too.

International problems are simple compared to the difficulties in a home with three teenagers and one phone.

If only men took the nation's problems as seriously as they do its sports!

The world has so many problems that if Moses had come down from Mount Sinai today, the two tablets he carried would be aspirins.

The problem the average housekeeper faces is that she has too much month left over at the end of the money.

Our problems are man-made; therefore they may be solved by men. And man can be as big as he wants. No problem of human destiny is beyond human beings.
                                                        —*John F. Kennedy*

You've got a problem when your dentist tells you that you need a bridge, and you can't pay his toll.

The right angle to approach a difficult problem is the "try-angle."

If you could kick the fellow responsible for most of your problems, you couldn't sit down for three weeks!

Sign on a chaplain's desk: "If you have troubles, tell me about them. If you don't, tell us how you do it."

Responsibility

There are no benefits without burdens, no freedom without responsibility.   —*Bert Rauch*

Admission: I have a very responsible job here; I'm responsible for everything that goes wrong.

Too many people get their exercise by jumping to conclusions, running up bills, stretching the truth, bending over backward, lying down on the job, side-stepping responsibility, and pushing their luck.

Man blames most accidents on fate—but feels personally responsible when he scores a hole-in-one.

The buck stops here.   —*Harry S. Truman*

Some men grow under responsibility, while others only swell.

Government is like a baby: an alimentary canal with a big appetite at one end and no sense of responsibility at the other.   —*Ronald Reagan*

When you take responsibility on your shoulders, there isn't much room left for chips.

Give responsibility to young men. Let them make their mistakes early. The good ones will learn from their mistakes.   —*A. Lightfoot Walker*

The price of greatness is responsibility.
                                        —*Winston Churchill*

Privilege and responsibility are two sides of the same coin.

He who buries his talent is making a grave mistake.

The ability to accept responsibility is the measure of the man.   —*Roy L. Smith*

You cannot help men permanently by doing for them what they could and should do for themselves.
                                        —*Abraham Lincoln*

Responsibility is my response to God's ability.
                                        —*Albert J. Lown*

It's an awesome responsibility to own a Bible.

Freedom is a package deal—with it comes responsibilities and consequences.

A duty which becomes a desire will ultimately
become a delight.   —*George Gritter*

No one does his duty unless he does his best.
                                        —*Billy Sunday*

Few things help an individual more than to place
responsibility upon him, and to let him know that
you trust him.   —*Booker T. Washington*

Self-Control

It is better to be slow-tempered than famous; it is
better to have self-control than to control an army.
                             —*Solomon (Proverbs 16:32)*

To stay out of hot water, keep a cool head.

Keep your mouth shut and your IQ will go up.
—*Murray Pezim*

The best way to save face is to keep the lower part shut.

A man without self-control is as defenseless as a city with broken-down walls.   —*Solomon (Proverbs 25:28)*

A man's conquest of himself dwarfs the ascent of Everest.   —*Eli J. Schiefer*

Be careful of your thoughts, they may break into words at any time.

He who talks without thinking runs more risks than he who thinks without talking.

I never preach religion to my players, but I won't tolerate profanity. This isn't for moral reasons. Profanity to me symbolizes loss of control; self-discipline is absolutely necessary to winning basketball.
—*John Wooden*

A rebel shouts in anger; a wise man holds his temper in and cools it.   —*Solomon (Proverbs 29:11)*

He who thinks twice before saying nothing is wise.

One sure way to test your self-control is to see a
friend with a black eye and not ask any questions.

Self-control means controlling the tongue! A quick
retort can ruin everything.   —*Solomon (Proverbs 13:3)*

The best time to keep your shirt on is when you're
hot under the collar.

Men who live without self-control are exposed to
grievous ruin.

If you speak when you're angry, you'll make the best
speech you'll ever regret.

Anger is momentary madness, so control your
passion or it will control you.   —*Horace*

Poise is the act of raising your eyebrows instead of
the roof.

A wise man controls his temper. He knows that
anger causes mistakes.   —*Solomon (Proverbs 14:29)*

He that would govern others first should be the
master of himself.   —*Philip Massinger*

The man who masters himself is delivered from the force that binds all creatures. —*Goethe*

When angry, count to ten before you speak; if very angry, a hundred. —*Thomas Jefferson*

The best executive is the one who has sense enough to pick good men to do what he wants done, and self-restraint enough to keep from meddling with them while they do it. —*Theodore Roosevelt*

Those who wish to transform the world must be able to transform themselves. —*Konrad Heiden*

But I will write of him who fights
And vanquishes his sins,
Who struggles on through weary years
Against himself and wins. —*Caroline Begelow LeRow*

The man who loses his head is usually the last one to miss it.

At no time is self-control more difficult than in time of success.

Self-reverence, self-knowledge, self-control, these three alone lead life to sovereign power.
—*Alfred, Lord Tennyson*

Self-control is giving up smoking cigarettes; extreme self-control is not telling anybody about it.

Self-control might be defined as the ability to carry a credit card and not abuse it.

If a man keeps his trap shut, the world will beat a path to his door.

Silence

Even a fool is thought to be wise when he is silent. It pays him to keep his mouth shut.
—Solomon (Proverbs 17:28)

Silence is evidence of a superb command of the English language.

To sin by silence when they should protest makes cowards out of men.   *—Abraham Lincoln*

Some people won't suffer in silence because that would take the pleasure out of it.

He who is a man of silence is a man of sense.

Wisdom is made up of ten parts, nine of which are silence—the tenth, brevity.

He who does not understand your silence will probably not understand your words.
—*Elbert Hubbard*

It doesn't do to do much talking when
you're mad enough to choke,
For the word that hits the hardest is
the one that's never spoke.
Let the other fellow do the talking
till the storm has rolled away,
Then he'll do a heap of thinking 'bout
the things you didn't say.

I have never been hurt by anything I didn't say.
—*Calvin Coolidge*

If silence is golden, not many people can be arrested for hoarding.

It is better to be silent and be considered a fool than to speak and remove all doubt.

Absolute silence—that's the one thing a sportswriter can quote accurately. —*Bobby Knight*

You must speak up to be heard, but sometimes you have to shut up to be appreciated. If there's a substitute for brains, it has to be silence.

Where's the manly spirit of the truehearted and the unshackled gone? Sons of old freemen, do we but inherit their names alone? Is the old pilgrim spirit quenched within us? Stoops the proud manhood of our souls so low that mammon's lure or party's wile can win us to silence now? Now, when our land to ruin's brink is verging, in God's name let us speak while there is time: now, when the padlock for our lips is forging, silence is a crime.

—*John Greenleaf Whittier*

Silence isolates us from the crowds that love to pool their misery; an unhappy civilization is always gregarious.   —*Fulton J. Sheen*

If you rest your chin in your hands when you think, it will keep your mouth shut so you won't disturb yourself.

In silence man can most readily preserve his integrity.

—*Meister Eckhart*

Talking comes by nature; silence by wisdom.

In Maine we have a saying that there's no point in speaking unless you can improve on silence.

—*Edmund Muskie*

Luigi Tarisio was found dead one morning with scarce a comfort in his home, but with 246 fiddles which he had been collecting all his life, crammed into an attic, the best in the bottom drawer of an old rickety bureau. In very devotion to the violin, he had robbed the world of all that music all the time he treasured them; others before him had done the same, so that when the greatest Stradivarius was first played it had had 147 silent years.

Discretion is putting two and two together and keeping your mouth shut.

At no time is it easier to keep your mouth shut than during an audit of your income-tax return.

Silence is the best and surest way to hide ignorance.

People who can hold their tongues rarely have any trouble holding their friends.

If you don't say anything, you won't be called on to repeat it.

—*Calvin Coolidge*

The hardest thing to keep is quiet!

It's funny how people on a diet are never reduced to silence.

A wise man is one who has an open mind and a closed mouth.

Keep your mouth closed and you'll stay out of trouble.   —*Solomon (Proverbs 21:23)*

Silence is
the only thing that cannot be misquoted;
something rarely found in men, women and children;
another thing that marriage brings out in a man;
sometimes golden, and sometimes just plain yellow;
the best way for a man to express his contempt,
      especially when the other man is bigger.
Blessed is the man who, having nothing to say,
abstains from giving wordy evidence of the fact.
                                             —*George Elliot*

If you keep your mouth shut, you won't put your foot in it.

None preaches better than the ant, and she says nothing.   —*Benjamin Franklin*

Another nice thing about being speechless is that you won't be picked to head a committee.

No one has ever repented of having held his tongue.

True silence is the rest of the mind.   —*William Penn*

A closed mouth catches no flies.

Sincerity

Lord, who may go and find refuge in your tabernacle up on your holy hill?

Anyone who leads a blameless life and is truly sincere. Anyone who refuses to slander others, does not listen to gossip, never harms his neighbor, speaks out against sin, criticizes those committing it, commends the faithful followers of the Lord, keeps a promise even if it ruins him, does not crush his debtors with high interest rates, and refuses to testify against the innocent despite the bribes offered him—such a man shall stand firm forever.   —*Psalm 15*

Sincerity—a silent address.   —*Oliver Goldsmith*

Loss of sincerity is loss of vital power.
                              —*Christian Nestell Bovee*

Sincerity—to practice more than your tongue says.

The only guide to a man is his conscience; the only
shield to his memory is the rectitude and sincerity of
his actions.   —*Winston Churchill*

The primary condition for being sincere is the same
as for being humble: not to boast of it, and probably
not even to be aware of it.   —*Henri Peyre*

Fear the LORD and serve Him in sincerity and truth.
                              —*Joshua (24:14, NASB)*

We are not sent into this world to do anything into
which we cannot put our hearts.   —*John Ruskin*

Sincerity—being yourself in any direction.

I want to see you shoot the way you shout.
                              —*Theodore Roosevelt*

Sincerity makes the least man to be of more value
than the most talented hypocrite. —*Charles Spurgeon*

A blush is one thing that can't be counterfeited.

What is uttered from the heart alone will win the
hearts of others to your own.   —*Goethe*

The devil is sincere, but he is sincerely wrong.
                                        —*Billy Graham*

Be sincere and without offense till the day of Christ.
                    —*The Apostle Paul (Philippians 1:10)*

Prayer must mean something to us if it is to mean
anything to God.

Be suspicious of your sincerity when you are the
advocate of that upon which your livelihood depends.
                              —*John Lancaster Spalding*

Sincerity needs no witnesses.

Of all the evil spirits abroad at this hour in the world,
insincerity is the most dangerous.
                              —*James Anthony Froude*

The kindling power of our words must not come
from outward show but from within, not from
oratory but straight from the heart.
                                   —*St. Francis de Sales*

Sincerity is the face of the soul.

Sincerity—an openness of heart.   —*La Rochefoucauld*

Success

Success is to be measured not so much by the position that one has reached in life as by the obstacles which he has overcome while trying to succeed.
                                    —*Booker T. Washington*

The secret to success is to do the common things uncommonly well.   —*John D. Rockefeller, Jr.*

He who wants milk should not sit on a stool in the middle of the pasture expecting the cow to back up to him.

Success is a journey, not a destination.
                                    —*Ben Sweetland*

A man who refuses to admit his mistakes can never be successful. But if he confesses and forsakes them, he gets another chance.   —*Solomon (Proverbs 28:13)*

When success turns your head, you're facing failure.

Sometimes it is not good enough to do your best;
you have to do what's required.   —*Winston Churchill*

Success is the ability to hitch your wagon to a star
while keeping your feet on the ground.

Accept the challenges, so that you may feel the
exhilaration of victory.   —*George Patton*

Success is facing up to a no-win situation—and
winning anyway.

Lincoln's Road to the White House
Failed in business in 1831
Defeated for legislature in 1832
Second failure in business in 1833
Suffered a nervous breakdown in 1836
Defeated for Speaker in 1838
Defeated for Elector in 1840
Defeated for Congress in 1848
Defeated for Senate in 1855
Defeated for Vice President in 1856
Defeated for Senate in 1858
Elected President in 1860

Did you hear about the fellow who climbed the
ladder of success wrong by wrong?

A man rarely succeeds at anything unless he has fun doing it.

A successful man is one who can lay a firm foundation with the bricks that others throw at him.
                                        —*David Brinkley*

You don't have to lie awake nights to succeed—just stay awake days.

Success humbles the great man, astonishes the common man and puffs up the little man.

The *Los Angeles Times* described a Beverly Hills barber's career as a case of "climbing the lather of success."

Man owes his success to two people: his wife and the Joneses.

Isn't it a shame that when success turns a man's head it doesn't wring his neck at the same time?

Success is relative—the more success, the more relatives.

Success is getting what you want; happiness is wanting what you get.

Success that goes to your head usually pays a short visit.

If at first you don't succeed, avoid skydiving.

Recipe for success: Study while others are sleeping; work while others are loafing; prepare while others are playing; and dream while others are wishing.
—*William A. Ward*

If at first you don't succeed, you're running about average.

Success is the child of audacity.   —*Benjamin Disraeli*

He who wants to finish the race must stay on the track.

The Lord has given us two ends,
they have a common link;
For with the bottom end we sit,
and with the other think.
Success in life depends upon
which end you choose to use.
You'll soon discover this, my friend,
Heads you win and tails you lose!

This year's success was last year's impossibility.

It takes twenty years to make an overnight success.
                                                    —*Eddie Cantor*

One of the biggest troubles with success is that its recipe is often the same as that for a nervous breakdown.

Success often comes from taking a misstep in the right direction.

You have reached the pinnacle of success as soon as you become uninterested in money, compliments or publicity.   —*Eddie Rickenbacker*

The secret of success is to be like a duck—smooth and unruffled on top, but paddling furiously underneath.

Becoming number one is easier than remaining number one.   —*Bill Bradley*

He who wakes up and finds himself successful has not been asleep.

Even a woodpecker owes his success to the fact that he uses his head.

All the roads to success are uphill.

There are three rules for success: the first is—Go on.
The second is—Go on. And the third is—Go on!
> —*Frank Crane*

President Schwab of Bethlehem Steel said that success was ten percent ability; ten percent appearance; five percent availability; five percent adaptability; and seventy percent attitude.

If you want to be successful, it's just this simple:
Know what you're doing. Love what you're doing.
And believe in what you're doing. —*Will Rogers*

Success defies the law of gravity; it means climbing to the top of the ladder by staying on the level.
> —*O. A. Battista*

That man is a success who has lived well, laughed often and loved much; who has gained the respect of intelligent men and the love of children; who has filled his niche and accomplished his task; who leaves the world better than he found it, whether by an improved poppy, a perfect poem or a rescued soul; who never lacked appreciation of earth's beauty or failed to express it; who looked for the best in others and gave the best he had.
> —*Robert Louis Stevenson*

It's not a successful climb unless you enjoy the journey.   —*Dan Benson*

You will find the key to success under the alarm clock.

There are no secrets to success. It is the result of preparation, hard work, and learning from failure.
                              —*Colin L. Powell*

Success is never final and failure never fatal. It's courage that counts.   —*George Tilton*

The father of success is work—the mother of achievement is ambition.

A lot of people owe their success to advice they didn't take.

Tact
(also Diplomacy)

Silence is not always tact, and it is tact that is golden, not silence.   —*Samuel Butler*

A quick and sound judgment, good common sense, kind feeling, and an instinctive perception of character, in these are the elements of what is called tact, which has so much to do with acceptability and success in life.   —*C. Simmons*

A diplomat can keep his shirt on while getting something off his chest.

If you can pat a guy on the head when you feel like bashing it in, you're a diplomat.

Tact is changing the subject without changing your mind.

Being diplomatic is telling your boss he has an open mind instead of telling him he has a hole in the head.

A diplomatic husband said to his wife, "How do you expect me to remember your birthday when you never look any older?"

Diplomacy is the art of taking sides without anyone knowing it.

You never know till you try to reach them how accessible men are; but you must approach each man by the right door.   —*Henry Ward Beecher*

A smile is the magic language of diplomacy that even a baby can understand.

Tact comes as much from goodness of heart as from fineness of taste.   —*Endymion*

A diplomat is a parent with two boys on different Little League teams.

Tact is the ability to describe others as they see themselves.   —*Abraham Lincoln*

A diplomat remembers a lady's birthday but forgets her age.

Let us never negotiate out of fear, but let us never fear to negotiate.   —*John F. Kennedy*

Diplomacy is the art of saying "Nice doggie!" until you can find a stick.

In order to be a diplomat one must speak a number of languages, including double-talk.
                                    —*Carey McWilliams*

Diplomacy: The art of jumping into troubled waters without making a splash.   —*Art Linkletter*

Talent is something, but tact is everything. Talent is serious, sober, grave, and respectable; tact is all that, and more too. It is not a seventh sense, but is the life of all the five. It is the open eye, the quick ear, the judging taste, the keen smell, and the lively touch; it is the interpreter of all riddles, the surmounter of all difficulties, the remover of all obstacles.

—*W. P. Scargill*

Diplomacy is the art of letting someone else have your way.

In the battle of existence, talent is the punch; tact is the clever footwork.   —*Wilson Mizner*

Tact is the art of making a point without making an enemy.   —*Howard W. Newton*

Some people mistake weakness for tact. If they are silent when they ought to speak and so feign an agreement they do not feel, they call it being tactful. Cowardice would be a much better name.

—*Sir Frank Medlicott*

Time

People, people everywhere,
Pushing, rushing here and there.
Laughing, talking, wasting time,
Playing, basking in sunny clime.
Where are you going?
What is your goal?
Where is your heart?
Where is your soul?
Time's swiftly passing,
Judgement is near.
People are wailing
In sorrow and fear.
Precious moments
So fruitless and lost.
What have you gained?
What has it cost?   *—Stephen J. Earl*

I have so much to do today that I shall spend the first
three hours in prayer.   *—Martin Luther*

When God wants to grow a squash He grows it in
one summer; but when He wants to grow an oak He
takes a century.   *—James A. Garfield*

The Moving Finger writes; and having writ
Moves on: nor all
your Piety nor Wit
Shall lure it back to conceal half a Line,
Nor all your Tears wash out a Word of it.
—Edward Fitzgerald

To everything there is a season, and a time to every
purpose under the heaven.
—Solomon (Ecclesiastes 3:1, KJV)

If you think time heals everything, try waiting in a
doctor's office.

Time is so powerful it is given us only in small doses.

Those who make the worst use of their time are the
first to complain of its shortness. *—Jean de la Bruyére*

Insurance salesman: "Don't you want your office
furnishings insured against theft?"

Manager: "Yes, all except the clock. Everyone
watches that!"

Teach us to number our days aright, that we may
gain a heart of wisdom. *—Psalm 90:12 (NIV)*

A great timesaver is love at first sight.

By the time you get your shoulder to the wheel, your nose to the grindstone, and your ear to the ground, it's usually time for lunch.

Sign in New Zealand department store clock display: "There's no present like the time."

A city slicker driving through a small mountain town screeched to a halt and shouted to an old-timer sitting on a bench: "Hey, Rube! What time is it?"

"Twelve o'clock," replied the old man.

"Are you sure?" snapped the driver. "I thought it was later than that."

"Don't never get no later than that around here," drawled the old man. "When it gets to twelve, we start all over."

Counting time is not so important as making time count.

Sign on office bulletin board: "In case of fire don't panic. Simply flee the building with the same reckless abandon that occurs each day at quitting time."

Satan doesn't care how lofty your intentions may be as long as they're focused on tomorrow.

Take time to think—it is the source of power.
Take time to play—it is the secret of perpetual youth.
Take time to read—it is the fountain of wisdom.
Take time to pray—it is the greatest power on earth.
Take time to love and be loved—it is a God-given privilege.
Take time to be friendly—it is the road to happiness.
Take time to laugh—it is the music of the soul.
Take time to give—it is too short a day to be selfish.
Take time to work—it is the price of success.

Tomorrow is usually the busiest day of the year.

If you must kill time, work it to death.

Time is money.

—*Benjamin Franklin*

Sign over college classroom clock: "Time will pass; will you?"

He who kills time injures eternity.

Don't let yesterday use up too much of today.

—*Will Rogers*

Time is a versatile performer. It flies, marches on, heals all wounds, runs out, and will tell.
                                    —*Franklin P. Jones*

Why is there never enough time to do it right—but always enough time to do it over?

Factory sign: "If you have nothing to do, please don't do it here!"

One thing you can learn by watching the clock is that it passes the time by keeping its hands busy.

Since time flies, it's up to you to be the navigator.

We master our minutes, or we become slaves to them; we use time, or time uses us.

I recommend that you take care of the minutes, for the hours will take care of themselves.
                                    —*Lord Chesterfield*

Some people can stay longer in an hour than others can in a week.

Our days are identical suitcases—all the same size— but some people can pack more into them than others.

More time is wasted not in hours but in minutes. A bucket with a small hole in the bottom gets just as empty as a bucket that is deliberately kicked over.

Hard work means prosperity; only a fool idles away his time. —*Solomon (Proverbs 12:11)*

When as a child, I laughed and wept,
Time crept.
When as a youth, I dreamed and talked,
Time walked.
When I became a full-grown man,
Time ran.
And later, as I older grew,
Time flew.
Soon I shall find while traveling on,
Time gone.

Dost thou love life? Then do not squander time, for it is the stuff life is made of. —*Benjamin Franklin*

Life's road is rough but you can make it;
Hold out your hand and God will take it.

No matter how hard you try to improve on Mother Nature, you're not kidding Father Time. What Mother Nature giveth, Father Time taketh away.

Guard well your spare moments. They are like uncut diamonds. Discard them and their value will never be known. Improve them and they will became the brightest gems in a useful life. —*Ralph Waldo Emerson*

Most of our troubles stem from too much time on our hands and not enough on our knees.

Time is a circus always packing up and moving away.
                                        —*Ben Hecht*

The present is a point just passed.   —*David Russell*

Time goes, you say? Ah, no! Alas, time stays, we go!
                                        —*Henry A. Dobson*

Time
Take time to pray—it helps to bring God near and
    washes the dust of the earth from your eyes.
Take time to laugh—it is the singing that helps with
    life's loads.
Take time to love—it is the one sacrament of life.
Take time to dream—it hitches the soul to the stars.
Take time to worship—it is the highway to reverence.

What I do today is important because I'm exchanging a day of my life for it.

Slow Me Down, Lord!

Slow me down, Lord!
Ease the pounding of my heart by the quieting of my
   mind.
Steady my hurried pace
With a vision of the eternal reach of time.
Give me, amidst the confusion of my day,
The calmness of the everlasting hills.
Break the tension of my nerves
With the soothing music of the singing streams
That live in my memory.
Help me to know the magical restoring power of
   sleep.
Teach me the art of taking minute vacations of
   slowing down
To look at a flower,
To chat with an old friend or make a new one,
To pat a stray dog, to watch a spider build a web,
To smile at a child, or to read from a good book.
Remind me each day
That the race is not always to the swift,
That there is more to life than increasing its speed.
Let me look upward into the towering oak
And know that it grew great and strong
Because it grew slowly and well.   —*Orin L. Crain*

Time is the dressing room for eternity.

Time is but the stream I go a-fishing in.
                              —*Henry David Thoreau*

Trust

The highest pinnacle of the spiritual life is not joy in
unbroken sunshine, but absolute and undoubting
trust in the love of God.   —*A. W. Thorold*

Fear of man is a dangerous trap, but to trust in God
means safety.   —*Solomon (Proverbs 29:25)*

Trust men and they will be true to you; treat them
greatly and they will show themselves great.
                              —*Emerson*

As contagion
of sickness makes sickness,
contagion of trust makes trust.   —*Marianne Moore*

Love all, trust a few.   —*William Shakespeare*

A man is a fool to trust himself! But those who use
God's wisdom are safe.   —*Solomon (Proverbs 28:26)*

When you cannot trust God you cannot trust anything; and when you cannot trust anything you get the condition of the world as it is today.

—Basil King

Trust in the Lord with all your heart, and do not rely on your own insight.   *—Solomon (Proverb 3:5, RSV)*

Trust him little who praises all, him less who censures all, and him least who is indifferent about all.

—Lavater

To be trusted is a greater compliment than to be loved.   *—J. Macdonald*

Trust in God does not supersede the employment of prudent means on our part. To expect God's protection while we do nothing is not to honor but to tempt providence.   *—Quesnel*

An undivided heart, which worships God alone and trusts Him as it should, is raised above all anxiety for earthly wants.   *—Geikie*

Trust in your money and down you go! Trust in God and flourish as a tree!   *—Solomon (Proverbs 11:28)*

Understanding

Understanding
If I knew you and you knew me,
If both of us could clearly see,
And with an inner sight divine
The meaning of your heart and mine,
I'm sure that we would differ less,
And clasp our hands in friendliness;
Our thoughts would pleasantly agree
If I knew you and you knew me.   —*Nixon Waterman*

How much better is wisdom than gold, and understanding than silver!   —*Solomon (Proverbs 16:16)*

True fortitude of understanding consists in not suffering what we do know to be disturbed by what we
do not know.   —*Paley*

Husband's admission: "All right, you don't understand me. I don't suppose Mrs. Einstein understood
Albert either."

Understanding is the reward of faith.
                                    —*Saint Augustine*

The best way to be understood is to be understanding.

Knowing God results in every other kind of understanding.   —*Solomon (Proverbs 9:10)*

A theological student came to Charles Spurgeon one day, greatly concerned that he could not grasp the meaning of certain verses in the Bible. The noted English preacher replied kindly but firmly, "Young man, allow me to give you this word of advice. Give the Lord credit for knowing things you don't understand!"

Time which diminishes all things increases understanding for the aging.   —*Plutarch*

Humanity's greatest need is not for more money, but for more understanding.

Wisdom and good judgment live together, for wisdom knows where to discover knowledge and understanding.   —*Solomon (Proverbs 8:12)*

A simple rule in dealing with those who are hard to get along with is to remember that this person is striving to assert his superiority; and you must deal with him from that point of view.   —*Alfred Adler*

Let us have faith that right makes might; and in that faith let us to the end dare to do our duty as we understand it.   —*Abraham Lincoln*

There are two periods in a man's life when he doesn't understand women—before marriage and after marriage.

A father can give his sons homes and riches, but only the Lord can give them understanding wives.
                                          —*Solomon (Proverbs 19:14)*

Sandy Koufax, Dodger pitcher, discussing Casey Stengel: "When I was young and smart, I couldn't understand him. Now that I am older and dumber, he makes sense to me."

Despite the fact that man's limitless ingenuity has made it possible for the leaders of distant nations to contact each other in a matter of seconds, mankind still has a communications problem. Because real communication is based on understanding.
                                          —*Lawrence F. O'Brian*

One who understands much displays a greater simplicity of character than one who understands little.   —*Alexander Chase*

A clever man tells a woman he understands her—but a stupid one tries to prove it.

Great Spirit, help me never to judge another until I have walked two weeks in his moccasins.
                                        —*Sioux Indian prayer*

After being scolded by his parents, a little boy said to his sister, "I'll never understand grownups if I live to be eight!"

Most people believe they see and understand the world as it is. However, we really see it as we are.

He who calls in the aid of an equal understanding doubles his own.   —*Edmund Burke*

When rejecting the ideas of another, make sure you reject only the idea and not the person.

It is not the eye that sees the beauty of the heaven, nor the ear that hears the sweetness of music or the glad tidings of a prosperous occurrence, but the soul that perceives all the relishes of sensual and intellectual perfections; and the more noble and excellent the soul is, the greater and more savory are its perceptions.   —*Jeremy Taylor*

Our Lord opened the understanding of His disciples. He sought entrance for truth by that avenue. He does so still.   *—T. C. Hammond*

Vision

I see America, not in the setting of a black night of despair ahead of us; I see America in the crimson light of a rising sun fresh from the burning creative hand of God. I see great days ahead, great days possible to men and women of vision.   *—Carl Sandburg*

Where there is no vision, the people perish.
                          —Solomon (Proverbs 29:18, KJV)

Whoever it was who searched the heavens with a telescope and found no God would not have found the human mind if he had searched the brain with a microscope.   *—George Santayana*

Hundreds of people can talk for one who can think, but thousands can think for one who can see. To see clearly is poetry, prophecy, and religion—all in one.
                                          —John Ruskin

Vision is the world's most desperate need. There are no hopeless situations, only people who think hopelessly.   —*Winifred Newman*

Vision is the art of seeing things invisible.
                                              —*Jonathan Swift*

The amount of vision that dwells in the man is a correct measure of the man.   —*Thomas Carlyle*

The vision to see, the faith to believe, and the will to do will take you anywhere you want to go.

Visionary people are visionary partly because of the very great many things they don't see. —*Berkeley Rice*

A task without vision is drudgery; a vision without a task is a dream; a task with a vision is a victory.

Eyes that look are common. Eyes that see are rare.
                                              —*J. Oswald Sanders*

A rock pile ceases to be a rock pile the moment a single man contemplates it, bearing within him the image of a cathedral.   —*Saint-Exupéry*

A great mind is one that can forget or look beyond itself.   —*William Hazlitt*

Wisdom
(also Ignorance)

The first key to wisdom is assiduous and frequent
questioning. For by doubting we come in enquiry
and by enquiry we arrive at the truth. —*Peter Abelard*

The Lord grants wisdom! His every word is a treasure of knowledge and understanding. For wisdom
and truth will enter the very center of your being,
filling your life with joy.   —*Solomon (Proverbs 2:6,10)*

Wise men change their minds; fools never.

No man really becomes a fool until he stops asking
questions.   —*Charles P. Steinmetz*

"Integrity and wisdom: These are the keys to business success," the old man was telling his son. "By
integrity, I mean that when you promise the delivery
of merchandise on a certain day you must do so even
if it bankrupts you."

"Well," asked the son, "what is wisdom?"

"Don't make such promises."

How does a man become wise? The first step is to trust and reverence the Lord! Only fools refuse to be taught. Listen to your father and mother. What you learn from them will stand you in good stead; it will gain you many honors. —*Solomon (Proverbs 1:7–9)*

The door of wisdom swings on hinges of common sense and uncommon thoughts. —*William A. Ward*

Knowledge is a process of piling up facts; wisdom lies in their simplification. —*Martin H. Fischer*

Every young man who listens to me and obeys my instructions will be given wisdom and good sense. —*Solomon (Proverbs 2:1,2)*

Thinking well is wise;
Planning well is wiser;
Doing well, wisest of all.

The art of being wise is the art of knowing what to overlook. —*William James*

A wise teacher makes learning a joy; a rebellious teacher spouts foolishness. —*Solomon (Proverbs 15:2)*

The doorstep to the temple of wisdom is a knowledge of our own ignorance. —*Charles Spurgeon*

Some are wise, and some are otherwise.

For the Lord grants wisdom! His every word is a
treasure of knowledge and understanding.
                              —*Solomon (Proverbs 2:6)*

Everybody is ignorant, only on different subjects.
                              —*Will Rogers*

He who thinks education is costly ought to try
ignorance.

Wise men learn more from fools than fools from
wise men.   —*Cato the Censor*

There is nothing more frightful than ignorance in
action.   —*Goethe*

Stupidity is forever; ignorance can be fixed.

If 50 million people say a foolish thing, it is still a
foolish thing.   —*Anatole France*

So teach us to number our days, that we may apply
our hearts unto wisdom.   —*Moses (Psalm 90:12, KJV)*

A good deal of trouble has been caused in the world
by too much intelligence and too little wisdom.

A wise man's words express deep streams of thought.
—*Solomon (Proverbs 18:4)*

Intelligence: Spotting a flaw in the boss's character.
Wisdom: Not mentioning it.

If ignorance is bliss, why aren't more people happy?

I don't think much of a man who is not wiser today
than he was yesterday.   —*Abraham Lincoln*

It's a wise man who lives with money in the bank,
it's a fool who dies that way.   —*French proverb*

A fool is his own informer.   —*Yiddish proverb*

Who makes quick use of the moment is a genius of
prudence.   —*Johann Kaspar Lavater*

The wisest person is not the one who has the fewest
failures but the one who turns failures to best
account.   —*Richard R. Grant*

The wisdom of this world is foolishness to God.
—*The Apostle Paul (1 Corinthians 3:19)*

A fool tells what he will do; a boaster what he has
done; the wise man does it and says nothing.

A fool says, "I can't"; a wise man says, "I'll try."

The wise learn from tragedy; the foolish merely
repeat it.   —*Michael Novak*

Wisdom is often times nearer when we stoop than
when we soar.   —*William Wordsworth*

My son, honey whets the appetite, and so does wisdom! When you enjoy becoming wise, there is hope
for you! A bright future lies ahead.
                           —*Solomon (Proverbs 24:13,14)*

If wisdom's ways, you'd wisely seek,
Five things observe with care;
Of whom you speak, to whom you speak,
And how and why and where.

Knowledge is horizontal; wisdom is vertical and
comes from above.   —*Billy Graham*

Wisdom is the main pursuit of sensible men, but a
fool's goals are at the ends of the earth!
                           —*Solomon (Proverbs 17:24)*

Wisdom is knowing what to do next, skill is knowing
how to do it, and virtue is doing it.   —*David S. Jordan*

Before God, we are equally wise—equally foolish.
                                        —*Albert Einstein*

Nine-tenths of wisdom is being wise in time.
                                        —*Theodore Roosevelt*

He who is wise by day is no fool by night.

The wise are promoted to honor, but fools are
promoted to shame!   —*Solomon (Proverbs 3:35)*

When you have got an elephant by the hind legs and
he is trying to run away, it's best to let him run.
                                        —*Abraham Lincoln*

A wise man thinks all he says; a fool says all he thinks.

He who loves wisdom loves his own best interest
and will be a success.   —*Solomon (Proverbs 19:8)*

A wise husband will buy his wife such fine china
that she won't trust him to wash the dishes.

A wise man will never plant more garden than his
wife can take care of.

From the errors of others a wise man corrects his
own.   —*Publius Syrus*

Epitaph on Charles II
Here lies our Sovereign Lord the King,
Whose word no man relies on,
Who never said a foolish thing,
Nor ever did a wise one.
—John Wilmot, Earl of Rochester

The road to wisdom? Well, it's plain and simple to express:
Err, and err, and err again but less and less and less.
—Piet Hein

Wisdom is knowing less but understanding more.

Wisdom—common sense to an uncommon degree.

There are four kinds of people:
Those who know not, and know not that they know not.
These are foolish.
Those who know not, and know they know not.
These are the simple, and should be instructed.
Those who know, and know not that they know.
These are asleep; wake them.
Those who know and know they know.
These are the wise; listen to them.
—Arab philosopher

From a wise mind comes careful and persuasive
speech.   —*Solomon (Proverbs 16:23)*

As a man grows older and wiser, he talks less and
says more.

Caution is the eldest child of wisdom.   —*Victor Hugo*

Wisdom enables one to be thrifty without being
stingy, and generous without being wasteful.

When a man lacks wisdom
His mind is always restless, and his senses are wild
    horses
Dragging the driver hither and thither.
But when he is full of wisdom
His mind is collected
And his senses become tamed horses
Obedient to the driver's will.

Wise words are sometimes spoken in jest, but many
more foolish ones are spoken in earnest.

If you want to know what God wants you to do, ask
him, and he will gladly tell you, for he is always
ready to give a bountiful supply of wisdom to all
who ask him; he will not resent it.   —*James (1:5)*

Wonder
(also Awareness, Awe)

He who can no longer pause to wonder and stand
rapt in awe is as good as dead; his eyes are closed.
                                        —*Albert Einstein*

Wonder is the basis of worship.   —*Thomas Carlyle*

I have no fear that the candle lighted in Palestine
years ago will ever be put out.   —*William R. Inge*

I *am*—the power of self-knowledge;
I *think*—the power to investigate;
I *know*—the power to master facts;
I *feel*—the power to appreciate, to value, to love;
I *wonder*—the spirit of reverence, curiosity, worship;
I *see*—the power of insight, imagination, vision;
I *believe*—the power of adventurous faith;
I *can*—the power to act and the skill to accomplish;
I *ought*—the power of conscience, the moral
     imperative;
I *will*—will power, loyalty to duty, consecration;
I *serve*—the power to be useful, devotion to a cause.
                                   —*George Walter Fiske*

The man who cannot wonder ... who does not habitually wonder and worship, is but a pair of spectacles behind which there is no eye.

—*Thomas Carlyle*

Two things fill me with constantly increasing admiration and awe, the longer and more earnestly I reflect on them: the starry heavens without and the moral law within.

—*Immanuel Kant*

Men love to wonder, and that is the seed of our science.

—*Emerson*

The Extravagance of Man
More sky than man can see,
More seas than he can sail,
More sun than he can bear to watch,
More stars than he can scale.

More breath than he can breathe,
More yield than he can sow,
More grace than he can comprehend.
More love than he can know.

—*Ralph Seager*

Wonder, connected with a principle of rational curiosity, is the source of all knowledge and discovery, and it is a principle even of piety.

—*Horsley*

The larger the island of knowledge, the longer the
shoreline of wonder.   —*Ralph W. Sockman*

The world will never starve for want of wonders, but
only for want of wonder.   —*Gilbert Keith Chesterton*

A man gazing on the stars is proverbially at the
mercy of the puddles on the road.   —*Alexander Smith*

To be surprised, to wonder, is to begin to understand.
                                    —*Jose Ortega Y Gasset*

Work

I never did anything worth doing by accident, nor did
any of my inventions come by accident; they came
by work.   —*Thomas Edison*

The lazy man longs for many things but his hands
refuse to work. He is greedy to get, while the godly
love to give!   —*Solomon (Proverbs 21:25,26)*

Providence sends food for the birds but does not
throw it in the nest.

Most people work for a good cause: 'cause they need the money.

Actually, most people aren't afraid of hard work. They fight it year after year.

In time you may perhaps find that most of the work of the world is done by people who aren't feeling very well. —*Le Baron Russell Briggs*

The second-laziest worker on earth is the one who joined as many unions as he could, to make sure he was always on strike.

If you want a place in the sun, be willing to expect some blisters. —*Rob Hatten*

Work is the natural exercise and function of man . . . Work is not primarily a thing one does to live, but the thing one lives to do. It is, or should be, the full expression of the worker's faculties, the thing in which he finds spiritual, mental and bodily satisfaction, and the medium in which he offers himself to God. —*Dorothy L. Sayers*

Some people remind us of blisters; they show up after the work is done.

Hunger is good—if it makes you work to satisfy it!
                          —*Solomon (Proverbs 16:26)*

Our Lord does not care so much for the importance
of our works as for the love with which they are
done.   —*Teresa of Avila*

The difference between an amateur and a professional is this: An amateur hopes; a professional
works.   —*Oscar Hammerstein*

A turning wheel does not get rusty.

Poverty passes by a hard-working man's door.

The more you sweat in peace, the less you bleed in
war.
—*Chinese proverb used by General Norman Schwarzkopf
                  at Naval Academy graduation, 1991*

Hard work brings prosperity; playing around brings
poverty.   —*Solomon (Proverbs 28:19)*

Nothing is work unless you would rather be doing
something else.   —*William James*

A pint of sweat will save a gallon of blood.
                              —*George Patton, Jr.*

The supermarket bag boy was asked, "How long have you been working here?"

He replied, "Ever since they threatened to fire me!"

We have two classes in this country: the working class, and the one whose teacher has left the room for a few minutes. —*Frank Walsh*

Why is it that some people stop working as soon as they find a job?

Success is sweet, but its secret is sweat.

Let us be grateful to Adam our benefactor. He cut us out of the "blessing" of idleness and won for us the "curse" of labor. —*Mark Twain*

Soap, water and elbow grease; those are the three ingredients for success in the hotel business.
—*Conrad Hilton*

The only place where success comes before work is in the dictionary. —*Vidal Sassoon*

Far and away the best prize that life offers is the chance to work hard at work worth doing.
—*Theodore Roosevelt*

The life of an entrepreneur is full of sacrifice. Body builders have a saying, "No pain, no gain." That should be the credo of every entrepreneur.

—*Victor Kiam*

The desire to work is so rare that it must be encouraged wherever it is found.   —*Abraham Lincoln*

The reason worry kills more people than work is that more people worry than work.   —*Robert Frost*

There aren't any hard-and-fast rules for getting ahead in the world—just hard ones.

If you won't plow in the cold, you won't eat at the harvest.   —*Solomon (Proverbs 20:4)*

Salesmen: This machine will cut your work in half. Customer: Great! I'll take two!

A city boy spent his first night on a farm. Much earlier than usual, he was awakened by the activity around him. He remarked sleepily, "It doesn't take long to stay here all night, does it?"

My boss advised me to work eight hours and sleep eight hours—only it shouldn't be the same eight hours.

Don't knock the Puritan Ethic:
Hard work for hard work's sake.
With it they built a new nation
Without taking a coffee break!

The world is full of willing people; some willing to
work, the rest willing to let them.   —*Robert Frost*

I know hard work never hurt anyone, but I'm not
taking any chances.

Work never tires me. Idleness exhausts me
completely.   —*Sherlock Holmes*

He who wants to make footprints in the sands of
time must not sit down.

Most of us aren't really workaholics. Think about it:
Have you ever heard of a Thank-God-It's-Monday
Club?

A stranger came to three workmen all of whom were
employed on the same job. He asked each worker
what he was doing. Growled the first man: "I'm
breaking rocks." Said the second: "I'm earning a
living." But the third man replied with a smile, "I'm
building a cathedral."

No race can prosper till it learns that there is as much
dignity in tilling a field as in writing a poem.
                                        —*Booker T. Washington*

The more steam you put into your work, the louder
you can whistle when your work's done.

Here's a stubborn truth
On which you can bet:
The harder you work,
The luckier you get.   —*L. J. Huber*

The worst day of fishing beats the best day of work.

Leisure and I have parted company. I am resolved to
be busy till I die.   —*John Wesley*

He who wishes to eat in the evening must be willing
to work earlier in the day.

The trouble with a husband who works like a horse
is that all he wants to do in the evenings is hit the
hay.

Now I get me up to work;
I pray the Lord I may not shirk,
And if I die before tonight,
I pray my work will be all right.   —*Donald Sharp*

Confession: When I have the urge to work, I lie down until it goes away.

Many people who complain about being up to their ears in work are just lying down on the job.

He who cuts his own wood warms himself twice.

People were once so primitive that they did not know how to get money except by working for it.
—*George Ade*

Nowadays, both husband and wife are bringing home the bacon. The argument now is—who's going to cook it?

He who fiddles around seldom gets to lead the orchestra.

Although it may seem
That the process is slow,
Still, work is the yeast
That raises the dough.   —*Mary Hamlett Goodman*

Be thankful for the problems on your job! If you didn't have them, you would not be there; and if they were less difficult, someone with less ability would have your job.

Having a maid nowadays is not a status symbol. It means the wife is working.

The best way to hear money jingle in your pocket is to "shake a leg."

Little girl to mother: "If Daddy can't get his work finished at the office, why don't they put him in a slower group?"

He who can't cut the mustard should not pick up the knife.

A good thing to remember,
A better thing to do:
Work with the construction gang,
Not with the wrecking crew.

Too many people are ready to carry the stool when the piano needs to be moved.

The lazy man won't go out and work. "There might be a lion outside!" he says. He sticks to his bed like a door to its hinges! He is too tired even to lift his food from his dish to his mouth! Yet in his own opinion he is smarter than seven wise men.

—Solomon (Proverbs 26:13–16)

Most of this world's useful work is done by people who are pressed for time, or are tired or don't feel well.

Genius is about two percent inspiration and ninety-eight percent perspiration.   —*Thomas Edison*

It's difficult to soar with eagles when you have to work with turkeys.

I don't mind work if I've nothing else to do;
I quite admit it's true
That now and then I shirk
Particularly boring kinds of work, don't you?
But on the whole, I think it's fair to say,
Provided I can do it my own way,
And that I need not start today—I rather like work!

He who rolls up sleeves seldom loses shirt.

Do you know a hard-working man? He shall be successful and stand before kings!
                    —*Solomon (Proverbs 22:29)*

Work is the grand cure of all the maladies and miseries that ever beset mankind—honest work, which you intend getting done.   —*Thomas Carlyle*

To crush, to annihilate a man utterly, to inflict on him the most terrible of punishments so that the most ferocious murderer would shudder at it and dread it beforehand, one need only give him work of an absolutely, completely useless and irrational character.   —*Dostoevski*

Hard work means prosperity; only a fool idles away his time.   —*Solomon (Proverbs 12:11)*

He who does nothing renders himself incapable of doing anything; but while we are executing any work, we are preparing and qualifying ourselves to undertake another.   —*William Hazlitt*

Zeal
(also Enthusiasm)

I have never seen a man who could do real work except under the stimulus of encouragement and enthusiasm and the approval of the people for whom he is working.   —*Charles M. Schwab*

He who has no fire in himself cannot ignite others.

Be zealous for God; remember, more people chase
fire engines than ice carts!

An Indian, having heard from a white man some
strictures on zeal, replied: "I don't know about
having too much zeal; but I think it is better the pot
should boil over than not boil at all."

The world belongs to the enthusiast who keeps cool.
—*William McFee*

Enthusiasm is the key not only to the achievement of
great things but to the accomplishment of anything
that is worthwhile.   —*Samuel Goldwyn*

In things pertaining to enthusiasm, no man is sane
who does not know how to be insane on proper
occasions.   —*Henry Ward Beecher*

The apostles turned the world upside-down because
their hearts had been turned right-side up.

Awake, my soul! Stretch every nerve, and press with
vigor on; a heaven race demands thy zeal, and an
immortal crown.   —*Philip Doddridge*

The worst bankruptcy in the world is the person
who has lost his enthusiasm.   —*H. W. Arnold*

Spread your arms to those with needs, and serve
with joy and zest; fill each day with golden deeds,
and give your very best.   —*William A. Ward*

Enthusiasm extinguishes the gloom in the room.
                                   —*Frank Tyger*

Whatever you do, do it ardently. If necessary, get
used to getting up early and going to bed late. Never
leave any stone unturned. And if you only have one
hour to work with, make sure that what you do in
that hour is perfectly done. The old proverb makes a
lot of sense: "What is worth doing is worth doing
well." Energy and patience in business are two indispensable elements of success.   —*P. T. Barnum*

Nothing was ever achieved without enthusiasm.
                                   —*Ralph Waldo Emerson*

None are so old as those who have outlived
enthusiasm.   —*Henry David Thoreau*

Enthusiasm is a good engine, but it needs intelligence
for a driver.

Only passion, great passion, can elevate the human
soul to achieve great things.   —*Denis Diderot*

You have to hold on to time ... It passes all too
quickly, alas. You have to hold on to it [to] prevent it
from passing! And there is only one way to do that;
to find everything interesting, to be interested in
everything.   —*Sacha Guitry*

The fellow who is fired with enthusiasm for his
work is seldom fired by his boss.

A man will succeed at anything about which he is
really enthusiastic.   —*Charles M. Schwab*

Enthusiasm can achieve in one day what takes
reasoning centuries.

If it were as easy to arouse enthusiasm as it is
suspicion, just think what could be accomplished!

An enthusiast is a fellow who feels perfectly sure of
the things he is mistaken about.

Whenever we find ourselves more inclined to persecute than to persuade, we may then be certain that
our zeal has more of pride in it than of charity.
                                        —*Charles Caleb Colton*

Every production of genius must be the production
of enthusiasm.   —*Benjamin Disraeli*

Enthusiasm flourishes in adversity, kindles in the hour of danger, and awakens to deeds of renown.

Nothing is so contagious as enthusiasm.

The gap between enthusiasm and indifference is filled with failures.

A wise man once said that enthusiasm is nothing but faith with a tin can tied to its tail.

Zeal without knowledge is fanaticism.

Whatsoever ye do, do it heartily, as to the Lord, and not unto men.
                    —*The Apostle Paul (Colossians 3:23, KJV)*

.